The Insider's Guide to Supervising Government Employees

The Insider's Guide to Supervising Government Employees

KATHRYN M. JOHNSON

Editor

𝖨𝖨𝖨
MANAGEMENTCONCEPTSPRESS

MANAGEMENTCONCEPTSPRESS

8230 Leesburg Pike, Suite 800
Tysons Corner, VA 22182
(703) 790-9595
Fax: (703) 790-1371
www.managementconcepts.com/pubs

Printed in the United States of America

Library of Congress Control Number
2011936400

978-1-56726-326-8

10 9 8 7 6 5 4 3 2 1

ABOUT THE EDITOR

The idea for this book about supervising in government organizations was conceived by **Kathryn M. Johnson**. Kathryn has been a supervisor for over 30 years, 20 of which she spent in the federal government. Her intent was to create a book that offers government supervisors a way to think about and prepare for their important role of guiding others—in service of the public interest. She developed the framework and selected the areas of focus for *The Insider's Guide to Supervising Government Employees* based on their importance and relevance to effective supervisory performance. Through stories, she gives supervisors an easy way to connect with a broad range of supervisory experiences; the stories open up a wide variety of opportunities for government supervisors to add new learning and ideas quickly to support their own supervisory situations.

Currently, Kathryn is the Executive Director of the Leadership & Management Division at Management Concepts, a training and performance improvement company that focuses on serving the federal government. Her daily work involves creating learning and development experiences that help individuals at any level of an organization reach new levels of performance.

Previously, Kathryn gained her leadership and supervisory experience as an Air Force Officer in the United States Air Force and the Department of Defense. The depth and breadth of her responsibilities and exposure to many new and varied organizational environments, along with her insights into human development and the practice of leadership, have contributed to Kathryn's insider understanding of what it means to be an effective government supervisor.

Kathryn holds a BS from North Dakota State University, an MS from the Air Force Institute of Technology, and a Certificate in Leadership Coaching from Georgetown University. She is a Certified Acquisition Professional/Level III.

Contents

Preface

Effective supervisors are essential to the future of government. The knowledge, skills, and behaviors required to be an effective supervisor can come only through continuous learning and development.

There are many different ways to learn and develop as a government supervisor. *The Insider's Guide to Supervising Government Employees* offers one such opportunity, drawing from the rich and varied experiences of a broad range of people.

Some of the 32 contributors have had many years of experience; others just a few. Some made supervisory work their choice; others learned from their own supervisors. Some serve the public; others support the government through their life's work. Some have titles like program manager, facilitator, engineer, contracting officer, senior executive, human resource director, community organizer, lawyer, student, executive coach, politician, finance officer, administrative specialist, and IT manager. Some share their personal stories; others participated in work and learning experiences that gave rise to the sage lessons, promising practices, and new insights they share.

The result is a book of stories by and about supervisors as they experienced the many aspects of supervisory work and learned through those experiences. You can read the entire book over a weekend and put some new ideas into practice as the need arises on Monday. You can select a specific story or topic if you find yourself in a similar situation and need some ideas for taking your next step. You can also use the book as a source of ideas and inspiration to support the learning and development of a group of supervisors.

The Insider's Guide to Supervising Government Employees focuses on the essential elements for mastering the competencies and accountabilities of supervisory work in the government. It was compiled as a source of support to help you demonstrate your commitment to serving the public though your own effective supervision. The stories in this book are filled with helpful perspectives and ready-to-use practices for government supervisors—no matter what level you are serving in your department or agency and whether you are new to supervision, a practicing supervisor, or a senior executive supervisor.

A hands-on tool included in *The Insider's Guide to Supervising Government Employees* is a seven-step, 38-item Supervisor Readiness Assessment. Completing this self-assessment and the easy-to-use interpretation and planning tools will help you answer two key questions:

- How ready am I to supervise?
- How can I enhance my readiness to supervise?

We hope your reading and learning experiences will generate some new or different ideas about how to support others and make good things happen across the government.

As a government supervisor, you have the most important job in all of government. Make the most of it!

—*Kathryn M. Johnson*
September 2011

1

The Opportunity to Supervise

Making good things happen on a scale bigger than yourself is what supervision is all about.

As a government supervisor, you are the critical link between government directives and action. You have the greatest influence on the values, perspectives, work activities, engagement, and organizational alignment of others. You have the opportunity to implement the decisions of the President and Congress through the services your government organization provides to the American people.

Whether you are serving at the first level, middle level, or top level of your organization and you have others from within the organization reporting directly to you, your work is about accomplishing things through others. This direct reporting or supervisory relationship naturally creates variation and ambiguity because you are engaging with others to help make their work more efficient and effective. Balancing the tensions between the people aspects and the work aspects as you organize, guide, and support the work of others is what enables you to make good things happen and to ensure accountability for results.

You may be thinking: "I understand what supervision is, but how can I possibly be successful as a supervisor amid all the challenges I face in the government environment today? I have to deal with budget cuts; cumbersome processes for recruiting, workforce development, and knowledge sharing; resistance to change; poor performance; and low engagement and trust among individuals and groups."

Numerous studies conducted by government and nonprofit organizations over the past three decades have acknowledged these challenges as realities for government supervisors—and they are not going away anytime soon. *Yet there is a lot that you can personally do to influence how you show up and perform as a supervisor every day to elicit the best work from others.*

This first chapter is about creating a context for you to think about being a government supervisor. You will find stories written by or about supervisors who have learned through their experiences the importance of deciding whether supervision is right for them. You will also find guidance and ideas to ensure that you are ready to take on new and different supervisory challenges with both feet on the ground and a plan in hand, including a supervisor readiness self-assessment. Our hope is that the stories and self-assessment will enhance your understanding of what it means to be ready and to feel good about the work you accomplish through others.

More to Think About and Try

One thing we know for certain about effective supervisors is that they must have a healthy, good sense of others vis à vis their own selves. Yet, we do not have a word to capture this quality. Perhaps we could call it "otherish." How otherish are you?

IS SUPERVISING RIGHT FOR YOU?

To know if supervision is right for you, it is important to understand your motivations. I initially wanted to supervise others because I believed it was the only way to advance in my career. I assumed my career would follow a natural progression from individual contributor to supervisor. Making more money—which is typically the case as one advances into supervisory positions— didn't hurt either. Very quickly, though, I realized that these were the wrong reasons to want to be a supervisor. In my first supervisory position, I had to hire employees, fire employees, deal with performance issues, and work with a peer who had applied (but not been selected) for my position. After this experience, the next two positions I moved into were intentionally not supervisory positions.

Since that time, I have moved back into a supervisory position. This time, my motivations were entirely different. I truly wanted to lead others. I was ready and willing, and I even cherished the relationship building, the ups and downs of individuals' performance, the added responsibilities, and the pressure of having all eyes on me for guidance, support, leadership, and team performance. With a change in my motivations, I've taken a fresh look at my role as a supervisor, what others need and expect of me, and how I can be of service to them. Supervising is a different way of contributing. I still do "real" work, but first and foremost, my priority is to enable the success of others.

The only way to know if you want to be a supervisor is to try it out. Fortunately, you don't need to be promoted into a supervisory position to do so. Instead, look for opportunities to lead and to engage others in a variety of situations. Learn from each of these situations by taking the time to reflect on them before, during, and after the experience. Consider experimenting with supervising by:

- *Encouraging others.* Whether it is during a team project or in the most mundane of activities, give someone words of encouragement. How exciting is it for you to provide others a little wind in their sails?
- *Openly discussing performance.* With another individual, try to discuss the strengths of his or her performance as well as ways in which the individual could improve. If you are not currently a supervisor, consider talking openly with colleagues on project teams or peers. Provide direct, honest, helpful feedback, either positive or developmental.
- *Building trust.* Select a work relationship that may be strained and intentionally try to build trust. Work toward a mutual, win-win situation where you both feel better about the relationship.
- *Recognizing others for their contributions.* The act of having to think about someone else's performance and intentionally recognize a contribution is vital as a supervisor. Provide positive feedback or a small token of recognition; perhaps nominate someone for an award.

Regardless of which activities you engage in as you try to support others and create "experimental" supervisory situations, take the time to reflect on your experience. These situations will shed light on your interests and motivations to supervise others. The insights gained from this intentional experimentation and subsequent reflection will help you determine if you are excited by the idea of supervising—or if you're not.

More to Think About and Try

- Ask yourself if you are more excited by helping others do the work or by doing the work yourself. If you like the work you are doing, what would you gain by changing your position?
- Careers evolve. Being a supervisor at one point in your career does not mean you'll choose to be a supervisor for the rest of your career. Conversely, turning down a supervisory opportunity at one point in your career doesn't mean you can't be a supervisor at another point in your career.

QUESTIONS TO ASK BEFORE SAYING YES TO A NEW SUPERVISORY OPPORTUNITY

Any new venture or relationship involves surprises—some pleasant, others not. While it is never possible to predict the future, you can take a great deal of uncertainty out of the equation by asking some simple yet powerful questions before you agree to a new supervisory opportunity.

Over the years, I have gathered a list of questions that I use to help me decide if a supervisory opportunity I am considering is right for me. (Sometimes aspiring supervisors hesitate to ask these questions for fear of what the answers will reveal.) I have found that the best sources for answers are both formal and informal connections with people in the organization or the specific work unit I am considering.

The next time you are considering a new supervisory opportunity, seek out answers to these questions to help you make the right decision:

- What do you see as the biggest challenges and opportunities in the work unit you would be supervising?
- What is the history, the story, of this (part of the) organization?
- How are goals set? Do they meet the standard of SMART goals (specific, measurable, attainable, relevant, timely)?
- How is the organization changing and how might that affect the work unit you would be supervising?
- What is the current culture in the work unit? What adjectives would you use to describe it, both positive and negative?
- What is the turnover rate in the work unit? Why?
- What was the story with the last supervisor? How long was he or she in the position?
- What are your immediate supervisor's biggest opportunities or challenges?

THE FIRST THINGS YOU DO AS A SUPERVISOR SEND BIG MESSAGES

The first steps you take as a supervisor are important and highly visible. The first things you say and do send big messages that set expectations and may remain in the memories of others far longer than you might like. Choose your first steps wisely.

"I still remember the first gathering you had when you took over the division." These were the words I shared with my former supervisor when we crossed paths some years later. As I look back, I recall hoping that I would be as effective as he was when I took my first steps as a supervisor.

Some things I learned from my supervisor's first steps that I find useful when taking on new supervisory responsibilities include:

- **Resist the temptation to tell people "Here's how it's going to be around here from now on."** Such messages elicit an instant negative reaction and will make your job as a supervisor harder.
- **Decide on a few key messages.** Consistency and clarity will help everyone as they start to compare notes. It is good to address what will be happening as you settle in, what the organization is going through and how that relates to your group's work, some guiding principles you hold, and above all, an indication that you would like to hear directly from them how they think things are going. This message sows important seeds for your transition period (which generally lasts about 90 days).
- **Let them know your roles and responsibilities.** It is not really about you; it is about your roles and responsibilities as a supervisor of the work unit. They want to hear it from you.
- **Show them what a great listener you are becoming.** Ask questions and then let employees do the talking. This sends a key message that you care about their ideas and that you are going to be someone they can work with.
- **Outline the near-term future.** Let everyone know what they can expect in terms of future communication and interaction.

More to Think About and Try

- When thinking about your first steps as a new supervisor, always take time to plan and prepare for your first important exposure.
- After the first week, reflect on how you performed as you took over your new supervisory challenge; be critical in assessing how well you connected with your work unit.
- Get feedback from others to ensure that you have an accurate sense of how your employees are feeling.
- Continue to challenge yourself to get better with each new supervisor opportunity. Apply the lessons from the past, but always keep in mind that each work unit is unique.

SUPERVISING WELL TAKES TIME

Most people would readily agree that doing anything complicated— and doing it well—takes time. Those who study human performance take this as a given. You simply don't become an athlete overnight or master software coding in one sitting.

So why do so many supervisors say they don't have the time to do their jobs right?

"I don't have the time to listen to everybody."

"I don't have the time to explain this to the team."

"I don't have the time to conduct high-quality performance evaluations."

"It's faster if I just do it myself."

The clock ticks at the same rate for everyone, but we each choose how to spend our time differently.

As anyone who has ever written down all dollars spent (or calories consumed) for a month knows, our perception is not always 100 percent consistent with reality. A starting point for supervisors who don't think they have the time to supervise well is to get clear on how they are really spending their time. You may be surprised to find you are wasting time that could be spent actively supervising your employees.

Let's say you discover you have 15 minutes a day to devote to supervision. The real reason you're not taking advantage of that time may be that you're not exactly sure what to do next. Or supervising may make you uncomfortable.

With this insight and self-awareness, you can take some proactive steps in your available time to learn the basics of supervision: communication, goal-setting, and feedback, for starters. Most organizations simply throw supervisors into their new role, with no real preparation or learning. If this is the case, the ball is in your court.

In my first role as a supervisor, I was given zero training; as a result, I started off with the notion that my main job was to tell people what to do. Painful experience and a supervisor who encouraged me to use this approach only as a last resort jump-started my own learning as a supervisor.

The best way to learn is to continually experiment and notice clearly your results. Don't expect perfection right away. Supervising well takes time and experience. Feeling like you should already be proficient as a supervisor can cause helplessness and can sidetrack you from engaging in the steps you need to take to improve.

In honing your supervisory skills, it is important not only to focus on immediate goals but also to think about growth—of people, processes, teams, and organizational maturity. Don't make everything about right now; make a conscious effort to think about the future. Continuing to take steps in the right direction, over a sustained period of time, builds surprisingly powerful capability.

Also, be on the alert for a tendency to spend time in the weeds as a technical, solo performer. This is a predictable retreat for supervisors who are uncomfortable with the complexity, messiness, and social skills needed to supervise well. Overwhelmed by this all-new reality, it is easy to drop back to what you do well individually. If you let yourself slip into this comfort zone, you're not acting as a supervisor; instead, you're an individual contributor with a supervisor title.

More to Think About and Try

- Be aware of how you are really spending your time.
- Use time as an ally in developing your skills and be intentional about creating a plan for learning.
- Be honest with yourself about whether you really enjoy the work of being a supervisor. Making the right decision will benefit everyone.

CONNECTING WITH NEW SURROUNDINGS

Change in the workplace is a common story these days. Any new environment can be as scary as it is exciting. You don't know the people and you don't know the organization. More to the point, you don't know how you're going to be treated or how successful you will be in your new role. If you think this seems daunting, know that this period of uncertainty won't last forever. Just like your first day of school, you'll soon learn how to navigate the new landscape easily.

For five years, Monica supervised a support team in a successful department of her organization. The roles and responsibilities of her team members were well-established and work routines were just that—routine. There were five team members who worked well together and knew exactly how to accomplish their work. The team ran like a well-oiled engine.

Monica was informed that some organizational changes were being made. She was placed in a similar supervisory role in a new department of the organization that she knew little about. The rest of her department was dispersed to other new organizations, with two moving to Monica's new department. Monica and these two employees now joined with others from across the company to form a team. This new team was focused on delivering a different type of service than her previous group, and the expectations were not entirely clear at the outset. She was now supervising a smaller team, leaving her and other team members to take on additional work responsibilities.

Monica was unsure of the new department's mission, and she wasn't familiar with the people or the projects being performed. Her first step was to assess the situation. She asked for clarity about her role and her supervisor's expectations. Armed with this perspective, she set out to get familiar with the work. Monica read project plans and reviewed any contract documentation she was able to get her hands on. She scheduled meetings with colleagues in the organization to learn more about their roles and active projects. Since her team was responsible for supporting the organization, she made sure to ask specifically about how she could help them conduct their work or manage their projects. She also provided them with information about her team and their experience, offering help wherever needed.

Communicating with others in the organization soon provided Monica with the information she needed to build a roadmap for success for herself and for her team. Being flexible to the new environment and engaging in open dialogue with others, she was able to chart a clear path to how her new department could best support the organization.

More to Think About and Try

- Just as you are grappling with and adjusting to new surroundings, so is your team. Some may be new to the group and others may just be dealing with the uncertainty of having a new supervisor. It's important to devote some time to learning about your team: Who are they? What kind of experience do they bring? What are their expectations of you?

- You set the vision and expectations for your team. Employees need to know where they're going and what their contribution will be. Provide stability to the team however you can—by establishing clear boundaries, creating a roles/responsibilities matrix, and formalizing processes, for example. This minimizes anxiety and helps reinforce each employee's contribution to the organization.

- Communication is vital for a team to feel a sense of belonging. Giving employees insight into the organization as well as opportunities to ask questions or make suggestions will go a long way toward making them feel valued. Check in with the members of your team regularly.

- Remember what was important for you in connecting with your new surroundings—that's what each member of your team also needs to feel a sense of security and stability for the future.

ONE SIZE DOES NOT FIT ALL

How often have you tried to apply an approach or technique you are very familiar with, only to find you have created all sorts of confusion for others? As you seek new and different experiences with individuals and groups in your organization, you will be tempted to use what has worked for you as a supervisor in the past. I learned the hard way that one size does not fit all.

For five years I supervised a group of eight individuals whose duties were to create intellectual properties for the organization. Each project had its own purpose and each of the individuals led his or her project in a highly individual fashion. Recognizing that each project had unique requirements, we accommodated great latitude in work styles. One project demanded hours of research offsite. Another project dealt with time-sensitive testing, so the team's office hours varied widely from day to day. Each of the professionals worked independently and communicated regularly to report on progress or challenges. No one person's work depended on the advancement or success of another's. No one had to approve or disapprove anyone else's work.

Each group member was highly motivated by the nature of the work. Each was a senior person who was aware that good work on his or her individual project could bring recognition in the organization and in the field.

My main duties were to obtain and allocate the resources necessary for each person in the group to achieve individual goals within the constraints of the organization, create and maintain the structure to keep communication flowing within and outside the group, and provide an environment that would foster the highest level of success. As a supervisor, I was more of a facilitator. I was often called in to act as a sounding board or to assist in moving some element of a project forward—but never to establish day-to-day tasks or roles for the individuals. The less structure I imposed on each individual and the group as a whole, the better the group worked and the greater their accomplishments.

One of the projects was deemed successful enough to become a new practice for the organization. I left my group to lead the task force that was charged with implementing this new practice. My elation in spearheading the new endeavor was soon deflated by the problems I created when I tried to use the same supervisory techniques I had used with my last group—which had been so successful for me—with this new group.

The new group comprised 20 members, some salaried and some hourly, and included administrative staff, technicians, and personnel pulled from various departments throughout the organization. None had worked together before.

I made my first mistake at the initial meeting of the new group. I planned to use the meeting to set the general schedule, and I assumed that each group member would offer suggestions for how to accomplish the mission within the required time and costs. I had spoken to each person individually prior to the meeting and believed each knew his or her role. What I had not addressed before the meeting was how each of these folks would act within the group when they came together for the first time.

Many of the individual tasks were interdependent and I had not thought to create a matrix showing how each person was responsible for his or her portion of the complex tasks we had to accomplish as a group. My shortcomings quickly became apparent when one member—and then many others—asked, "So how is this going to work, exactly?"

For five years I had enjoyed success as a supervisor by keeping structure to a minimum. I tried to use what had worked for me in the past in this very different environment—and got off to a rocky start. This group needed structure. They had no history of working together, and they had no background with the new practice we were to implement.

Each new group, each new environment, and each new task requires a supervisor to consider the specific skills and techniques that will make the endeavor successful. Always try to keep in mind that one size does not fit all.

More to Think About and Try

- With any change in resources, tasks, or the environment in which you work, you should reevaluate your role as a supervisor. Communicate any change in your role to others (above and below you) to ensure that they too understand that the current situation necessitates different actions.
- Chart how each member of your group contributes to the accomplishment of the task. The chart should clearly show the responsibilities and should be communicated to the group.

ARE YOU READY TO SUPERVISE?

Whether you are thinking about becoming a supervisor for the first time or are taking on a supervisory role in a new group or a new organization, one of the most important steps is to honestly assess your readiness to be a supervisor. Taking the time to assess your readiness will enable you to determine if this type of work—or specific situation—is right for you.

Completing this seven-step, 38-item self-assessment and the easy-to-use interpretation and planning tools will help you answer two key questions:

- How ready am I to supervise?
- How can I enhance my readiness to supervise?

Step 1: Assess Your Readiness to Supervise

- For each item, circle the option that most closely represents your view. Think about a variety of past situations, events, and circumstances as you make your choices.
- Once you have answered all the questions in a section, total your responses in each column of that section.
- Then, use those numbers to add up your section subscore and record it in the space provided to the left of the subscores.

Supervisor Readiness Assessment			
Understanding Yourself as a Supervisor	**Yes**	**Not Sure**	**No**
1. I am comfortable taking on additional responsibilities to perform non-technical or non-functional work.	3	2	1
2. I am drawn to situations where I can help others excel in their job.	3	2	1
3. Taking a leadership role feels natural to me.	3	2	1

Understanding Yourself as a Supervisor	Yes	Not Sure	No
4. I have a clear sense of my own strengths.	3	2	1
5. I am willing to engage in self-assessment to become a better supervisor.	3	2	1
6. I can visualize myself as a supervisor.	3	2	1
SUBSCORE (total the gray boxes to the right):_____			
Understanding Supervisor Roles	Yes	Not Sure	No
7. Holding conversations to help people find the answers to their problems or challenges is something that comes naturally to me.	3	2	1
8. I am comfortable helping others seek out experiences they find energizing or motivating.	3	2	1
9. I find it rewarding to work with a team to help them accomplish a common goal.	3	2	1
10. I am at ease taking charge of a situation by setting the right tone and sharing the right information.	3	2	1
11. It is natural for me to figure out what people are good at and then advise them about the right job or role for them.	3	2	1
12. I am drawn to situations where I can motivate others to meet an organization's mission.	3	2	1

Continued on next page

Understanding Supervisor Roles	Yes	Not Sure	No
13. I am comfortable creating well-thought-out plans that will be adapted as the situation changes.	3	2	1
14. It is rewarding to me when I find ways to help others do their jobs better or overcome challenges they face in their jobs.	3	2	1
15. I am at ease taking on temporary roles where I am accountable for maintaining or improving a team's performance.	3	2	1
16. I am comfortable helping others learn new things so that they can become more effective in their jobs.	3	2	1
SUBSCORE (total the gray boxes to the right):_____			
Getting the Best Work from Others	Yes	Not Sure	No
17. It comes naturally to me to give feedback to others in a way that is honest yet constructive.	3	2	1
18. I am comfortable addressing sensitive topics with others, such as poor performance or ineffective work practices.	3	2	1
19. I find it rewarding to build others' trust and confidence in me through my words as well as my actions.	3	2	1

Getting the Best Work from Others	Yes	Not Sure	No
20. I can instantly relate to people by finding common ground.	3	2	1
21. I am willing to view a situation from someone else's perspective.	3	2	1
22. I am at ease delegating tasks to others and ensuring that they understand and are accountable for those tasks.	3	2	1
23. I make effective decisions by understanding the situation, getting input, stating assumptions, developing options, and communicating the decision.	3	2	1
24. I am willing to address conflict in a team or work group so the team can better meet its objectives.	3	2	1
SUBSCORE (total the gray boxes to the right):_____			
Making Good Things Happen	Yes	Not Sure	No
25. Understanding my organization's priorities comes naturally to me.	3	2	1
26. I am comfortable encouraging others to ask questions to ensure they clearly understand what is expected of them.	3	2	1

Continued on next page

Making Good Things Happen	Yes	Not Sure	No
27. The importance of building strong relationships is intuitive to me.	3	2	1
28. I am comfortable trying to understand my work environment even though I realize it is sometimes out of my control.	3	2	1
29. I take responsibility when I make a mistake, viewing it as an opportunity to learn and to help others avoid the same mistake.	3	2	1
30. I am willing to ask others to share their observations and experiences.	3	2	1
31. I realize that plans must be reexamined as the situation changes, including technical challenges as well as team morale.	3	2	1
32. I am at ease bringing up someone's negative or counterproductive behaviors in a constructive manner.	3	2	1
SUBSCORE (total the gray boxes to the right):_____			
Supervising in a Changing Work Landscape	Yes	Not Sure	No
33. I feel confident that I would understand the unique challenges of supervising employees in different work locations.	3	2	1
34. I am willing to learn more about using social media in a professional setting.	3	2	1
35. I am comfortable sharing information with others.	3	2	1

Supervising in a Changing Work Landscape	Yes	Not Sure	No
36. I embrace employees from different generations who have varying viewpoints about the workplace and how to get work done.	3	2	1
37. I know that to facilitate high performance, it is important to take into account how our minds work.	3	2	1
38. I am eager to constantly learn new skills and techniques and then try them out.	3	2	1
SUBSCORE (total the gray boxes to the right):_____			

Step 2: Total Your Subscores

Transfer your subscores for each section to the spaces provided below.

Questions 1–6	Questions 7–16	Questions 17–24	Questions 25–32	Questions 33–38
Understanding Yourself as a Supervisor	Understanding Supervisor Roles	Getting the Best Work from Others	Making Good Things Happen	Supervising in a Changing Work Landscape
_____	_____	_____	_____	_____

Step 3. Compile Your Results

Use your subscores for each dimension to shade Your Results. Here's an example of a shaded chart:

Sample Results

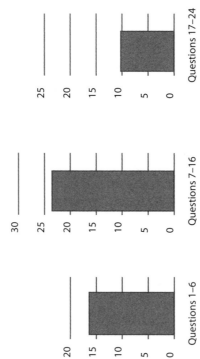
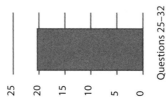

Your Results

	30 _____			
	25 _____	25 _____	25 _____	
20 _____	20 _____	20 _____	20 _____	20 _____
15 _____	15 _____	15 _____	15 _____	15 _____
10 _____	10 _____	10 _____	10 _____	10 _____
5 _____	5 _____	5 _____	5 _____	5 _____
0 _____	0 _____	0 _____	0 _____	0 _____
Questions 1–6	**Questions 7–16**	**Questions 17–24**	**Questions 25–32**	**Questions 33–38**
Understanding Yourself as a Supervisor	Understanding Supervisor Roles	Getting the Best Work from Others	Making Good Things Happen	Supervising in a Changing Work Landscape

Step 4: Interpret Your Subscores

Check off the subscore that matches your response for each of the five sections and read the corresponding text to interpret your responses. In Step 6 you will learn about some specific things you can do to enhance your readiness to supervise for each of the five dimensions of the readiness self-assessment.

Understanding Yourself as a Supervisor

If your subscore was...	Then read this text to interpret your responses:
☐ 6 – 9	You may not have a clear understanding of what supervision is about and who you are as a supervisor. Additional exposure would help you increase your understanding of what supervision means to you.
☐ 10 – 14	You have a good understanding of what supervision is and who you are as a supervisor, but you would benefit from learning more about what supervision means to you.

Continued on next page

Understanding Yourself as a Supervisor

If your subscore was...	Then read this text to interpret your responses:
☐ 15 – 18	You have a strong understanding of what supervision is and who you are as a supervisor. Consider further self-learning to deepen your understanding of what supervision means to you.

Understanding Supervisor Roles

If your subscore was...	Then read this text to interpret your responses:
☐ 10 – 16	You may have limited exposure or tend to avoid taking on some supervisory roles. You would benefit from learning more about each role to increase your effectiveness as a supervisor.
☐ 17 – 23	Your work responsibilities may have led to your awareness and comfort with many of the supervisory roles, but you may want to learn more about each specific role.
☐ 24 – 30	Your work exposure and comfort with the many roles of a supervisor give you a solid understanding of supervision. You could benefit from a more in-depth understanding of each supervisor role to enable you to make deliberate choices about appropriate roles in any supervisory situation.

Getting the Best Work from Others

If your subscore was...	Then read this text to interpret your responses:
☐ 8 – 13	You may not have a clear understanding of what it takes to get the best work from others. Additional exposure would increase your understanding of how to achieve results through others.

Getting the Best Work from Others

☐ 14 – 18	You have a good grasp of what it takes to get the best work from others, but may not always be consistent in applying what you know. There may be more for you to learn.
☐ 19 – 24	You have a strong idea of what it takes to get the best work from others, but you could improve your effectiveness by continuing to experiment with different approaches to working with others.

Making Good Things Happen

If your subscore was...	Then read this text to interpret your responses:
☐ 8 – 13	You may not be clear about how to make good things happen when supervising others. You would benefit from more exposure to this aspect of supervision.
☐ 14 – 18	You have a good idea of how to make good things happen when supervising others, but could improve your results through additional learning.
☐ 19 – 24	You have a strong sense of what it takes to make good things happen through others. You would benefit from new experiences to enhance your performance in this area.

Supervising in a Changing Work Landscape

If your subscore was...	Then read this text to interpret your responses:
☐ 6 – 9	You may not have much insight into how the work landscape is changing. You would benefit from learning more about how government supervisors are being asked to drive performance while dealing with the increased pace, scope, and complexity of work in their organizations.

Continued on next page

Supervising in a Changing Work Landscape

If your subscore was...	Then read this text to interpret your responses:
☐ 10 – 14	You have a basic understanding of how work and the workplace are changing, but you may not have spent much time delving into how your approach to supervising government employees will be affected.
☐ 15 – 18	You have a solid understanding of the new demands on government supervisors, but you would benefit from learning more about how to effectively guide, develop, and support others within the context of the new and emerging work environment.

Step 5: Prepare to Enhance Your Readiness to Supervise

Look at the subscores you checked above. Your next step is to decide how you want to enhance your readiness to supervise. In the space provided below, write down your top three priorities. You will use these priorities to create an action plan for enhancing your readiness to supervise.

My Top Three Priorities

Priority #1:
Priority #2:
Priority #3:

Step 6: Identify Ways to Enhance Your Readiness to Supervise

There are many different ways to enhance your readiness to supervise. Take a few minutes to read through the suggestions for each supervisor readiness dimension. Choose the suggestions that will help you meet your top three priorities and record them in your action plan in Step 7. You may have some ideas of your own that you would like to try as well.

Understanding Yourself as a Supervisor

Knowledge	Read Chapters 1 and 2 of *The Insider's Guide to Supervising Government Employees.* Ask others how supervision has worked for them. Check out the supervisory and leadership training opportunities at www.managementconcepts.com
Observation	Identify one or more supervisory situations to learn how personal values affect a supervisor's performance.
Practice	Record one or more interactions with others; analyze how you sound (e.g., tone, clarity, speed). Try using stories to help you get your point across to others. Practice supervising yourself, focusing on how you get work done.
Reflection	Keep notes on your thoughts about supervision, what you have to offer as a supervisor, and your areas of discomfort. Think of someone who is an effective supervisor. How are you similar to or different from this person?

Understanding Supervisor Roles

Knowledge	Read Chapter 3 of *The Insider's Guide to Supervising Government* Employees.
Observation	Learn from your supervisor by identifying the specific roles he or she used in one or more situations. Identify what worked and what didn't work.

Continued on next page

Understanding Supervisor Roles

Practice	Choose a supervisor role; find a seasoned supervisor to give you feedback after observing you practice the role.
Reflection	Identify experiences where you have performed some supervisory roles and reflect on what you learned about yourself. Imagine performing a specific supervisory role and record your thoughts.

Getting the Best Work from Others

Knowledge	Read Chapter 4 of *The Insider's Guide to Supervising Government Employees.* Seek out best practices from seasoned supervisors.
Observation	Identify one or more supervisory situations to see if you can identify the specific behaviors and techniques that brought out the best in other people.
Practice	Practice basic skills of listening, asking questions, and giving constructive feedback. Practice giving praise, saying thank you, and acknowledging great work.
Reflection	Note how your supervisors have gotten the best work out of you. Keep a journal of ideas you want to test.

Making Good Things Happen

Knowledge	Read Chapter 5 of *The Insider's Guide to Supervising Government Employees.* Seek best practices that other supervisors have used to break down barriers to getting work done.
Observation	Identify one or more supervisory situations to check your understanding of planning, leading, and coordinating specific work tasks.

Making Good Things Happen

Practice	Plan and facilitate a meeting that begins and ends on time. Visually and mentally rehearse something you want to try. Practice telling a person what you need from them and asking how they would approach the situation.
Reflection	Jot down notes on how you approach solving problems and making decisions. Think of a time when you felt good about supporting others to achieve a specific result.

Supervising in a Changing Work Landscape

Knowledge	Read Chapter 6 of *The Insider's Guide to Supervising Government Employees*. Check out articles, books, and presentations posted on the web about the changing work environment.
Observation	Identify one or more supervisory situations where you can experience working with remote workers or multiple generations.
Practice	Create a continuous learning plan that includes specific areas you want to learn more about as they relate to the changing work landscape.
Reflection	Create a list of all the things that are currently changing the work environment and think about how those factors will affect you as a supervisor.

Step 7: Develop Your Supervisor Readiness Action Plan

Record each activity you want to pursue from Step 6 in the first column of your readiness action plan. Then set a timeframe for completing each activity and record it in column 2. Use column 3 to note the specific people who can support you in completing the activity. Remember to review your action plan periodically to check your progress, add any new activities, or close out any completed activities.

Supervisor Readiness Action Plan

Actions I Plan to Take	By When?	How Others Can Support Me
For example: *Find at least five opportunities to practice asking questions so I get more comfortable considering the perspectives of others.*	*60 days from now*	*One person I will seek out is a colleague I have had a difficult time connecting with.*

2

Looking Inside, Understanding Yourself

How many times have you said to yourself, "I wish I had paid more attention to _____"?

Undoubtedly, you could come up with many words to fill in the blank. For this chapter, we have chosen the word "myself" to complete the sentence because the focus will be on you, the supervisor.

Looking inside—paying attention to and appreciating what you know and don't know as well as what is working well or not working well for you—is an important first step toward being able to guide and support others. The behaviors you demonstrate and the actions you take as a supervisor are indicators of how you respect yourself. This display of self-respect in turn contributes to the respect you show others.

The stories in this chapter are about some the most important aspects of getting to know and understand who you are and, more specifically, who you are as a supervisor. We consciously draw your attention to how your thinking, emotions, and responses to different circumstances affect you and those around you. We focus on such topics as visualizing yourself as a supervisor, understanding your strengths, being honest with yourself, and sharing stories as a way for others to learn about you. You will also get a glimpse into the many lessons that supervisors who have walked in your shoes have learned over their careers. We hope you will take away some insights and ideas to think about and perhaps try as you uncover what it means for you to be your best self as a supervisor.

HOW DO YOU VISUALIZE YOURSELF AS A SUPERVISOR?

We all visualize, whether we realize it or not. To illustrate, close your eyes and try to recall a recent experience that involved a variety of physical sensations (for example, walking on your favorite beach, running a race, or eating at a new restaurant). Try to create an image in your mind of the experience using all your senses (seeing, hearing, smelling, touching, tasting), your feelings, and your emotions. Try to recall as many details of the experience as you can. You have probably done this hundreds of times without realizing it.

While visualizing an experience that has already happened can help you understand it better, visualizing can have even greater value when you use it to create a picture in your mind of something that has not yet happened—exactly as you want the picture to be—with the intent that it will actually happen.

When I was a new supervisor, I recognized after the fact that the picture I had created in my mind about what I wanted to achieve as a new supervisor led to my early success. I have continued to get a lot of value from visualizing different situations before they occur. I liken it to "prep work" when encountering a new situation.

Although it was not my first job in the federal government, it was my first opportunity to consider the possibility of becoming a supervisor. I was assigned to a team dedicated to supporting the procurement of products and services for a field organization. It was a very busy job, particularly in the months leading up to the end of the fiscal year. I had been in this job for about three years when I learned that my supervisor was interviewing for an opportunity with another civilian agency. I found myself wondering what it would be like to be selected as the person to replace my current supervisor. I felt I was ready to take the big step of becoming a supervisor.

I started to formulate an image of what it would mean to be a supervisor in this organization. I had learned a lot about supervising by observing other supervisors—the good things and the not-so-good things they did. I felt I had a good understanding of what it would take to fit into this new role. I knew about the constant change we were experiencing, the many interruptions my supervisor handled while trying to keep the flow of work in balance, and the diverse roles I saw other supervisors performing. I knew I would have to continually keep myself from getting bogged down by all the day-to-day activities.

I also recognized that others had formed views of me over the past three years and that all eyes would be on me if I stepped into this new role. I kept thinking about more details. I knew I wanted to share my philosophy of leading and managing others as soon as I assumed my new role. I thought about the key points I wanted to make to my new team. I still remember them today: "Make service the focus of our actions and behaviors." "Get things done by working together." "Build on the strengths of each person." "Show personal leadership every day." I knew I needed to take some time to prepare for this first meeting. I envisioned preparing for it like I had done for other key events by setting aside some time over several days to test my message to make sure it was clear.

Knowing I would not be able to visualize everything I would experience as a new supervisor—and that I am not perfect—I thought about using a technique I learned from one of my past supervisors. The technique was to set aside time each day to reflect on what was happening. I knew it would be hard to keep this up, but I thought I'd give it a try.

Another thing I learned from a past supervisor that I wanted to make my own was to solicit and capture feedback as a way to continue to improve while helping others learn. I decided that every time I engaged with someone I would try to remember to close the conversation by asking "What is going well today?" and "What could be different?" I realized it would take some time to integrate this approach into the flow of conversations until it felt natural. I wanted to see if this worked for me.

I did get the job and I was able to put many of my thoughts into action. Looking back on this first supervisory experience as well as others that followed, I can clearly see how valuable it has been for me to create mental pictures of myself in different situations. As a supervisor, you will always encounter situations that challenge you. If you can visualize yourself in the situation before you are actually in it, you will find that you are able to integrate yourself into the new situation more quickly and confidently.

Whether you are an aspiring or an experienced supervisor, you have a new group to supervise, or you are facing a new supervisory situation, how do you visualize yourself as a supervisor?

More to Think About and Try

- If visualizing is new to you, an easy way to get started is to create a picture in your mind of what you want to be, have, or achieve as a supervisor. Be very specific. Take time to write out as many details as possible to help you clarify your thinking. What qualities will help get you where you want to be? What contextual factors will influence what you want to have? Who can support you in achieving your goal? When will you know that you have reached your goal?
- Once you become comfortable with visualizing yourself in different situations, it will be a natural way for you to prepare yourself to face new challenges. If you can visualize yourself in a situation, you can become your best self in that situation.

DO YOU HAVE A CLEAR SENSE OF YOUR OWN STRENGTHS?

Have you ever had a moment when you doubted your abilities? Have you ever made a mistake that shook your self-confidence? Did anyone ever tell you that you don't have what it takes to get something accomplished?

If you have found yourself in these situations, rest assured that you're not alone. Everyone has felt this way at one time or another. We tend to be hard on ourselves and lose confidence when something doesn't go the way we hoped. You've probably heard the saying, "you're your own worst critic." We tend to be harder on ourselves than we are on anyone else.

We take for granted the things we do well because they come easily. However, most people remember and even dwell on what isn't working. We tend to focus more on our shortcomings than our strengths.

The question is, how fast can you bounce back from this feeling of inadequacy? How resilient can you be? To regain your self-confidence, you may need to shift your thinking to a new paradigm. A tried-and-true approach is to remind yourself of what you do well. You have abilities, skills, and talents that you've proven time and time again. Think about those moments in your career when you demonstrated your professional capabilities. What was the context? What did you do well? How did you make it happen? What competencies did you apply to the situation?

Reflect on your entire professional career. Identify your successes, big and small. Perhaps you were recognized by your supervisor and other employees and received an award for your accomplishment. Or maybe it was a small achievement that only you knew about. The point is, you had to apply your strengths, skills, and knowledge to the situation to make it work.

As a supervisor, you're responsible for your staff as well as yourself. People are counting on you to do your best. Your ability to manage people and projects is critical. Supervision is often called a "soft skill." However, there's nothing soft about it; it's hard to supervise well because there are so many variables. You're dealing with people and their needs, values, work styles, preferences, and expectations, which don't always converge.

What are the strengths of a successful supervisor? One of my best bosses asked for my input and included me in decision-making, especially when it involved my responsibilities. I felt valued, that what I contributed mattered. He recognized me and other staff members for going above and beyond, and told each of us how much he appreciated our efforts.

Early in my career when I was a supervisor at a chain of community newspapers, I recognized the strengths of my staff, which I thought were being underutilized. I worked closely with the graphic artists to enliven the visual aspect of the papers, creating a more updated look. I asked the staff for their ideas. I listened to their suggestions and concerns—and let them know what I could and couldn't do. I expressed my appreciation for the improvements they made and highlighted the positive impact they had on the entire organization.

More to Think About and Try

- *Identify your strengths.* Make a written inventory of your jobs and projects, as well as the contributions you've made during your career. Ask your colleagues and friends what they think your strengths are and how you demonstrate them. Consider asking people you don't always agree with; they may provide an interesting perspective.
- *Consider using one or more of the many self-assessments on the market to help you identify your top strengths and ways you can put those strengths into action.* The more you know and understand about yourself and your strengths, the more effective you will be as a supervisor.
- *Find out how other people see your strengths.* Ask them to complete a 360-degree feedback survey. This survey is completed anonymously and focuses on your strengths as well as areas for development. Keep the list of positive comments about your strengths handy so you can review it when you're feeling unsure of yourself.

- *Keep your strengths in mind when you face a difficult situation.* Visualize the times you were at your best. What skills and talents did you apply to those circumstances? Then generate the energy to reinvigorate those abilities.
- *Don't be afraid to experiment.* How can you apply your strengths to something you feel passionately about to help you become a stronger supervisor? Perhaps you can take on a project or volunteer for a committee working in that area.

DO YOU KNOW HOW OTHERS SEE YOU?

On any given day there are many opportunities for others to observe you. They will take away a thought, an image, or possibly an idea about you as an individual. These takeaways may or may not be to your liking as they can be positive or negative. One example of a positive takeaway is when you display a strength that others readily notice about you.

Once you discover what your strengths are, you can leverage them in your personal and professional life. By doing this, I was able to see myself and others in a new way. I learned that my affinity for meeting new people is a strength referred to as WOO (Winning Others Over). I finally understood why members of my team often ask me to make introductions—they recognize my WOO. By realizing that WOO is a strength and is something that not everyone does well, I am able to help my team gain access to resources that help them be more effective.

A 50-year-old association was in jeopardy of folding. The same five volunteers had kept the association afloat for over 10 years, and they were worn out. A fellow colleague recommended that I help revitalize the chapter. My initial response was, "Who, me?" She convinced me that I could bring new energy to the organization by introducing new members and enlisting new volunteers. With some trepidation, I took her up on the suggestion. After a few challenging months, I was able to mobilize a new five-person board and double the membership numbers by Winning Others Over.

One strategy worked particularly well for me and my new team. As part of our weekly staff development meetings, we read *Now, Discover Your Strengths* by Marcus Buckingham and Donald O. Clifton (Free Press, 2001). After completing the assessment, we discovered that our five-person team had a range of strengths with few overlapping themes. These findings served as the basis for a team-building exercise as we began to understand the strengths of each member on the team and could tap into them when needed. Through this experience, we all gained key insights about each other's strengths, which led to an understanding of roles and responsibilities and a greater appreciation of the value that each person brought to our important work.

More to Think About and Try

- To gain insights about yourself and the collective team, take the initiative and do the work to discover how to leverage the strong points among your team that complement your own strengths. Pick up a copy of either *Now, Discover Your Strengths* or *StrengthsFinder 2.0* by Tom Rath (Gallup Press, 2007) for your team. Reading either book as a group and taking the online assessment will expose the team to a larger pool of themes or strengths; it also may be easier for each person to accept and appreciate the themes/strengths when observed in others.

- Find productive ways of receiving feedback from others to ensure that your words and actions are being perceived as intended.
- Pay attention to cues like silence, puzzled looks, missed deadlines, and sloppy work, as they may be indications of how others are responding to your communications, behaviors, or actions. Always remember that the opportunity to open up or shut down others begins with you.

DO YOU KNOW HOW TO GET THE BEST OUT OF YOURSELF?

It is often easier to give your attention to something other than yourself. However, to be at your best when supporting others, you must first know how to get the best out of yourself. As a supervisor, you will face many situations that will require you to muster up enough strength to get through, only to find another situation waiting to be addressed. The better you know and understand yourself, the easier it will be for you to be at your best while supporting others in working toward their goals.

How well do you know and understand yourself and what you bring to work every day? Do you know what gives you energy? Do you know what causes you to lose focus? Do you have a clear sense of your own strengths and limitations? Is there something about you that others always notice? Is there something about you that makes others uncomfortable? Do you know what it takes to propel you to a new level of insight, learning, and performance? Do you know how to create a spark in others so they can do their best work?

Addressing these questions will give you greater insights into how you can bring your best self to each supervisory situation. Over the years, I have found a variety of ways that help me understand myself, unlearn things that no longer serve me well, and find new ways to adapt to new and changing environments.

During a year-long mid-career professional development program, I had the opportunity to reflect on my supervisory experiences through several assignments. One assignment in particular stands out because I was asked to identify the things that have helped me get to know myself on a deeper level. I came to realize that while the opportunity to supervise is not unique, how I prepare myself for that opportunity is unique to me, as is what I bring to every supervisory situation. I learned a lot from the assignment. Each of the following learning points has become a guidepost for me as I continue to build my supervisory strength and try to bring my best self to each supervisory situation:

- **Reach out to experience new things.** I have raised my hand and often sought out opportunities to help me learn about something new or different. These experiences have helped me become more comfortable with change. They have also helped me appreciate that there is often more than one way to get things done.
- **Keep an open mind.** When I do not keep an open mind to listen and hear the views of others in challenging situations, I feel drained physically and emotionally. I feel like my brain is on mute. When I remember to step back and check my feelings, it becomes easier for me to refocus on the situation with a more open mind.

- *Recognize your choices.* I am keenly aware that my interests and experiences influence how I see and interpret situations, but I have also learned that I can choose to change the way I think about a situation. Once I came to appreciate that I have choices, it became easier to work through issues quickly and with better outcomes.

- *Listen on a deeper level.* As a supervisor, it is easy to get distracted and feel overwhelmed by the many things going on at the same time. It is also easy to get lazy about using good listening skills. Even though my first supervisory training exposed me to the value of putting aside my own thoughts, opinions, and history—and really trying to hear what the other person is trying to convey—at times I still catch myself not listening with intent.

- *Be curious and experiment.* When in a new supervisory situation, I find I am naturally curious and want to use my energy to find the best solution. I am not afraid to try new ways of doing things or to initiate little experiments to see what happens. I use questions to connect with others, uncover new information, and clarify understanding.

You will face the choice about what to do, how to act, and who to be in every supervisory situation. If you have a clear understanding of how you can bring your best self to your role as a supervisor, it will be easier for you to make decisions, take action, and respond to whatever comes your way.

More to Think About and Try

Three questions can help you gauge how well you know and understand yourself:

- Can you describe your thinking patterns?
- How do you interpret information?
- How do you interact with others?

These questions may seem pretty simple, but if you take a little time to delve deeper into each, you will likely surface some new insights into what is working for you and what you would like to change. I find that it works best for me to do this kind of self-reflection a little at a time. The break in time enables me to see a clearer picture of what I am trying to understand better or in a new way.

MAKING AND KEEPING PROMISES

There are many ways to gain or lose trust as a supervisor; one of the fastest ways to lose the trust of others is to make promises you can't keep. I have learned some things over the years as a government supervisor that have helped me get better at making and keeping promises.

My first big awareness came after I had been supervising project teams for about five years. A colleague I respected a great deal said to me after a meeting (in which I had agreed that my team would be the first group to launch a new software tool), "You look exhausted and now you have this new pressure on you. You need to take care of yourself or you won't be any good to anyone."

Saying "yes" was my way of showing senior leadership that I supported the initiative, but I knew the offer to be the first team to launch would put a lot of stress on my team. We would have to shift a lot of other projects, and I didn't even know if it was possible to make all the changes that would be necessary. As I was driving home from work that night, my colleague's words kept coming back to me; by the time I arrived home, I was feeling I had made a promise I would not be able to keep. I took a few minutes before starting dinner to write down things we would need to address to be able to launch the software tool; this made me feel even more unsettled. I decided to sleep on it and see how I felt in the morning.

The alarm went off and I was quick to get out of bed because I was going to do something I find to be a balance-maker in my life—a quick run on my favorite weekday running path. Once on the trail, I knew my thoughts would go right to my dilemma. The first thought that came to me was about why I had stepped into the situation. The running time to think helped me get to the place I needed to be when I arrived in the office. I suggested to my supervisor that all the team leads get back together to talk through the best approach for launching the software tool to minimize the impact on the teams and to help us get to full implementation.

The learning that took place as a result of my colleague's warning has stayed with me. While I am certainly better about making promises today, I have come to appreciate that I will always need reminders to help me avoid overpromising.

As a supervisor, you will have many occasions to make and keep promises—to yourself and others. If you are clear about your priorities, what you value as important, and what it takes to make things happen, you will win the trust of others and be able to keep the promises you make to yourself.

More to Think About and Try

- *Be open-minded.* Just as there are two sides to every coin, there are two sides to making promises. One side of the promise coin is you and the other side of the promise coin is others. Once I began to look at making promises from this perspective, it became easier for me to see the full impact of the promises I was making. I also learned that when I looked at only one side of a situation, I did not get the best outcome for all.

- *Realize that you can't please everyone.* Have you ever been told you are a pleaser? I have, and I have come to realize that this quality is at the core of what causes me to make promises I am not always able to keep. While being a pleaser connects to my basic value system and the importance I place on helping and supporting others, I have had to learn how to keep this quality in check so I do not overcommit myself.

- *Understand your intentions when making a promise.* If you are clear about why it is important to make the promise, you will be able to fully and genuinely make a commitment. Your hesitations will go away and you will be able to focus on making the promise a reality. When my thoughts, feelings, and behaviors are all aligned, I know the right things will happen.

- *Break the promise or goal into smaller, more manageable pieces* to minimize surprises. "Chunking" a project will enable you to see, check, and show progress toward achieving the promise. It also keeps you from feeling overwhelmed. With smaller pieces, it is easier to check in periodically on what you intend to deliver.

If you find it is not possible to keep a promise, you will be in a better position to raise the issue early, consider the consequences, and if appropriate, renegotiate the promise.

- **Seek support from others** to help you be accountable for keeping your promises. Routinely seek the help of others to help you continue to learn about yourself in new and different supervisory situations and how you will respond when you need to make a promise.

LEARNING TO SAY "I DON'T KNOW"

Saying "I don't know" is difficult for many supervisors. Perhaps it makes you feel vulnerable, or maybe you fear that others will think you lack knowledge or experience. The truth is that no supervisor has all the answers, and learning to say "I don't know" can be one of your greatest strengths.

A few years ago, while working for a large government agency, I was asked to design a consolidated mail operation program. After months of planning and completing several business case analyses to justify the enormous expense of the proposed consolidation, I presented my findings to senior leadership. The good news was that I was given approval to move forward with the consolidation project. The bad news was that I had to find funding and make it available for the program. Even worse, I realized I had to tell my boss and my team that I had no idea how to reprogram funds from within the organization to support the project.

This was not my first rodeo in the government—I had successfully led many teams, projects, and programs over the course of my career. Nevertheless, I felt inexperienced and worried about how others would perceive me when I had to say those three little words… "I don't know." I was used to solving complex problems; rarely would I hem and haw over issues. Understanding that I had to lead a team and get the job done, I swallowed my pride and scheduled time to tell my boss about my quandary.

As it turns out, my boss had no idea how to reprogram funds either. He smiled and said "So, figure it out and tell us how it's done." I was relieved. Not knowing how to perform a task suddenly became less of an issue, and my focus immediately shifted to defining a path that was not well traveled.

As I reached out to others in my agency, I quickly learned that very few had successfully reprogrammed funds. I was not the only one who did not know! Some people told me we wouldn't be able to do it. Others said that past and current appropriations acts offered few examples and none presented the same level of complexity as my project.

To make a long story short, I started out by asking my organization's budget officer what needed to be done to reprogram the funds. Next, I talked with the budget analysis folks and our legal staff to gather their input. The path then led me to speak with people in accounting, who ultimately had to approve the reallocation of funds from several accounts into a single account. I also learned I needed to tell the organizational and sub-organizational budget officers that they were going to be directed to contribute funding to the project; we worked together to develop an algorithm for determining who would contribute and at what funding level.

I am happy to say that, in the end, my team and I carved out a path that worked. We were able to turn "I don't know" into successfully reprogramming enough funds to allow our organization to adopt a consolidated mail program.

More to Think About and Try

- Learn to get comfortable with saying "I don't know." Now that I have done it a few more times, I find people really respect me for being open and honest. I also find it is easier to get support from others.
- Find others who have done it before and ask for advice and lessons learned from their experiences. Be sure to talk with people at different management and functional levels because each will have a different perspective on what is critical to know and do.
- Write down what you don't know, followed by what you do know, so you can develop a more detailed plan to accomplish your goal. Taking this step will make you aware of gaps that need to be closed.
- As you execute on your plan, seek feedback from your stakeholders. Sort out the key points you have learned that can be integrated into the execution process. I have been successful in taking this step by email, by phone, and in person.
- Apply your own learning to help you say "I don't know" again when the next circumstance comes up and test your skills by helping others you suspect are struggling to say they don't know.

HOW DO YOU CONNECT WITH OTHERS?

Communicating is supposed to be easy when you speak the same language, but think back to all the times you made a comment to someone that he or she did not understand—or even took offense when that was certainly not your intention. The way we prefer to connect with people is unique to our own inclinations and habits.

I have been trying to figure out how best to reach my bright but challenging new employee, Mike.

I hired Mike a few months ago to fill a senior position on my team. He had extensive experience and was very professional in his interviews. I was sure he would be a great addition to the team, and he has definitely been a major contributor to some of the process upgrades we've implemented recently. I know he enjoys socializing with his coworkers because he attends our monthly happy hour events, but I want to make sure he feels comfortable coming to me if problems arise; I'm just not sure we're there yet.

I dropped by his desk the other day to catch up and see how he was doing. I tried to make casual conversation by asking about his weekend, but all I got out of him were noncommittal answers. He seemed nervous and worried that I was there asking questions, but I just wanted to make sure he was content with his work and doing well. He seemed to want desperately to get back to work so I said goodbye quickly. It was awkward.

I mostly get one- or two-sentence emails from him with brief status updates on his progress. He doesn't seem to be interested in sharing anything but the bare minimum with me. I'm concerned that he is not happy with his job (I can't afford to lose someone with his experience), but I'm not sure how to correct the situation if he won't talk to me. I need to set up a one-on-one meeting with him, but I'd also like to engage in more casual communication to establish stronger rapport.

I was at a loss, so I asked Mike how he perceives the situation. This is what he shared:

I took a senior position on Cheryl's team a few months ago, and to be honest I still feel like I'm getting my sea legs. I like the work, but the pace here is much faster than what I'm used to, so I'm always scrambling to catch up. Cheryl stops by my desk pretty frequently, and I worry that she feels the need to check up on me because I'm doing something wrong or not meeting her expectations of how fast I work. I would love to take a minute to chat about my kids, but anytime I'm pulled away I get this nagging feeling that I'm going to miss my next deadline. I do make a point to go to happy hour to get to know my team better because I never have any time to chat at the water cooler—and I understand the importance of professional networking. I haven't had a chance to talk to Cheryl at happy hour yet because there are quite a few of us there; I guess I should make more of an effort next time.

Cheryl just put a meeting on my calendar for next week to catch up. I think I will share with her that things are going well but that I need to stay focused during the day to get my work done on time.

More to Think About and Try

- Even though Cheryl and Mike both recognize the need to strengthen their professional relationship, they struggle because they have different preferred styles for communicating and thus connect with people differently. The easiest way to head off "connection issues" is to determine together what your expectations are for the frequency and method of communication.
- Take the time to plan what and how you want to communicate. As a supervisor, Cheryl can clarify what work-related information she is looking for and when. In their upcoming one-on-one meeting, Mike also has an opportunity to share that he gets overwhelmed when he is distracted while working to meet a deadline, but that he's looking forward to catching up with Cheryl at the next happy hour.

> - If you find that you're struggling to connect with one of your employees, take a moment to ask them how they prefer to communicate. Be sure to clarify your expectations for how they should interact with you.

WHAT STORIES DO YOU SHARE?

Stories become part of our lives at a very early age and we make connections to them in our own unique ways. We hear stories. We create stories. We learn from stories. We share stories. Some stories stay with us longer than others. Some stories make us happy. Some stories make us angry. Some stories challenge us. Some stories change us in big ways. One particular experience completely changed how I receive and experience the sharing of stories.

I had just moved to a new community—my fourth government move in 10 years. I remember how hard the first couple of moves were, but as I look back on this fourth move, there was something very different about it. I immediately think about the book club I joined at the suggestion of my new neighbor. It was fall and the book club was coming back together after a summer break. There was an open space as one of the members had decided to drop out to finish her graduate work. The book club included men and women, all engaged in their career work across a wide variety of domains. For the first fall meeting, we were to pick our favorite children's book and tell the story to the other book club members. It was an easy choice for me: *Make Way for Ducklings*. Luckily, I had unpacked all my books so I could bring my well-worn copy with me to the meeting.

We all came away from the book club meeting with many reminders of the life lessons contained in the stories. But even more valuable to me was that this story-sharing experience helped me see personal transitions from a new perspective. I had found a quicker way to integrate into a new community.

Many times since this book club experience, I have used stories in other ways—to help make a new idea come to life, help others grasp a complex issue, or influence someone's views on a challenging topic. I have also come to realize that the stories I share as a supervisor are a direct reflection of who I am. It has been helpful for me to learn and put into to practice some good habits around choosing the stories I share, how I share them, and what I hope to achieve as a result of sharing them.

More to Think About and Try

- What kinds of stories do you share? Are they positive or negative? Do you share just the facts or do you add your own spin?
- Do you share stories about yourself? How do others respond to your personal stories?
- What kinds of stories do you tell over and over again?
- How often do you repeat stories you have heard from others?
- Do you take time to practice your story to make sure it flows and captures the attention of your listeners?

GETTING TO KNOW YOURSELF AS A SUPERVISOR

You can do many things both informally and formally to get to know yourself better as a supervisor. A good place to start is with some personal planning and being intentional about what is most important for you to know about yourself in a variety of situations. Here are some questions to spur your thinking:

- Would you like to understand more about your presence, how you make commitments, how you listen, how you make connections with others, or how you learn?
- Do you want to learn more about yourself in new or challenging situations, different kinds of meetings, one-on-one conversations, or dispersed work situations?
- What would you learn if you paid attention to what gives you energy, what disappoints you, and what causes you to lose patience?
- What do you see in others that you also see in yourself?
- How do you seek feedback from others? What feedback have you received that you didn't like? What did you do about it? How could you use feedback differently?
- What do you uniquely offer others? How would you describe yourself doing your best work?

The more you know about yourself as a supervisor, the easier it is to sense and predict your actions and reactions when circumstances change. Even more powerful is when you are able to move beyond gaining knowledge about yourself to exploring the basis of the knowledge, values, and attitudes that influence a particular supervisory situation to gain new insights into who you are as a supervisor.

More to Think About and Try

- What more do you want to learn about yourself?
- How do you want to learn more about yourself?
- Who could help you learn more about yourself?

3

The Power of Ten Supervisor Roles

How many different roles does a supervisor perform?

The list is longer than you might think. Whether you are a new or a seasoned supervisor, you will find yourself performing a variety of roles to support others.

In this chapter you will learn about ten key supervisory roles. We share stories by or about supervisors performing each of the ten roles. The intent of these stories is to help you learn through real work situations how a specific supervisory role plays out in the work environment. In telling their stories, those who have "been there, done that" share insights and ideas that will help you gain a better understanding of what a specific supervisory role involves—and what is important to remember when applying the skills associated with that role.

Following each story are some takeaways that you can put to use when you are preparing for or performing a specific supervisory role.

The most important thing to remember is that "the presenting situation" is what determines the initial roles a supervisor will play. As a situation unfolds, you may find it necessary to adjust or change the roles to improve the support you provide to help others achieve their desired outcome.

Once you are clear about the situation you are facing and what you are striving to accomplish, you will be ready to think about your most appropriate supervisory roles. Many supervisory roles call upon skills from specific domains such as coaching, facilitation, and leadership. It is helpful to learn what is unique about a specific role so you remain true to the intent of the domain when applying the related skills.

SUPERVISOR AS TALENT SCOUT

One of my best supervisors had a gift for selecting the right talent for the right work. In addition to her skill at considering each role in terms of the organization's current and future needs, Marcia was a generous, confident, coach-like leader who was not afraid to hire and develop employees with skill sets different from hers. She knew that in her role as a supervisor, it was important for her to create a team with complementary skills that met the organization's needs.

Marcia viewed talent management as a continuing part of her job, not just a task to complete when an opening arose on her team. She was a consummate networker who was actively engaged in various communities of professionals as a way to keep her eye out for the next great hire. I first met Marcia at a training course we both attended. Five years later, once I had earned the advanced degree we talked about during the course, she was one of the executives I reached out to in pursuit of a more challenging position. Marcia agreed to meet with me and continue networking regardless of whether our conversations led to a role on her team or not. Fortunately, they did.

Marcia delighted in seeing people succeed independent of their reporting relationship to her. One of my favorite project assignments came as a direct result of Marcia's willingness to give me a chance to work on an initiative to shift our organization's corporate culture. Aside from the knowledge and skills I developed during that time, I am to this day grateful for how Marcia stepped up for me as my supervisor and leader throughout that process. Part cheerleader and part sage, she gave me enough room to succeed without leaving me totally on my own. We established a schedule of check-in conversations at the start of the project so I could keep her informed along the way. She had an uncanny way of knowing when I might need more support or guidance from her.

I now realize that Marcia's keen intuition was only part of her skill. She took the time to assess what the project would involve compared to my level of experience—and she anticipated the places that would stretch me. She never presumed that I would need to call on her, yet she was always available as she expressed confidence in my ability to run the project by myself. It takes experience and confidence to become an effective "talent scout." It also takes humility, awareness of how people learn, and knowledge about the organization's needs to ensure that the right talent is in the right place at the right time.

More to Think About and Try

- *Craft an overall talent strategy.* Where is your organization going? What type of talent is required to get there? Craft a talent strategy in alignment with your mission. Map out where you are going to look for the right talent, when you are going to bring it on board, and what you will do to reduce the amount of time it takes each new hire to go from orientation to performance. Put milestones on your calendar to keep talent goals from being overtaken by the other tasks and deliverables that each supervisor must balance each day.

- ***Assess your current talent pool regularly in search of gaps and opportunities.*** Given your organization's strategic direction and goals, are the right people in the right roles right now—right for the organization and right for their unique combination of knowledge, skills, abilities, and interests? For example, do you have someone performing a role that she or your organization has outgrown? Look for another way to help that employee contribute that continues his growth and is still in service to the mission. If you have someone on your team who is underperforming in his role, take a fresh look at whether that person can reasonably acquire the knowledge, skills, abilities, and motivation he needs to perform to the organization's expectations. Don't forget that as a supervisor you play a key role in providing timely feedback and guidance to someone you believe has the capacity to become a solid performer.

- ***Don't delegate the role of talent scout.*** Talent scouts are proactive—they don't wait until someone submits his resignation or retirement to think about how they would fill a gap on their team. In addition to holding regular conversations with current members of your team, get out of your office on a regular basis. Stay engaged with your professional communities. When you network, remember that the next person you exchange business cards with may be the perfect fit for your team one day.

SUPERVISOR AS LEADER

As a supervisor, you never know when you may have to answer a call to step up to leadership. Managing others often presents you with situations you could never have anticipated, and sometimes those situations result from the actions of leaders above you.

As an administrative director in my organization, I answered to an executive director. This individual was a brilliant and passionate man. Unfortunately, his passion sometimes boiled over into frenzied excitement. While his exuberance often served to encourage my team, his actions at times alarmed them. One such instance occurred shortly after I joined the department. My team had spent nearly a year pursuing a very lucrative contract with a new customer. As in all contract negotiations, some days were better than others, and at one point in the process, even I began to wonder if we would come to mutual agreement on the contract terms.

It was during these difficult contract negotiations that my executive director proclaimed at a department-wide meeting one morning, "If we don't secure this contract, all of us could lose our jobs and our department will be disbanded within six months." That was not exactly the message I was hoping to send to my team, and I spent the rest of the day addressing my team's panic.

You never know when you will need to put on your "leader" hat. This experience taught me that perhaps my most important duty as a supervisor is to bring a sense of calm to an often chaotic environment. While I could not control the actions of senior leaders, I was responsible for setting the tone on my team. I learned to manage that leadership tone by adopting a few specific behaviors.

First, I began to make concerted efforts to ensure that my team was appropriately informed of developing events—both positive and negative—so they felt prepared to respond to or receive feedback from others on issues. Had I informed my team that the executive director was troubled by the state of the contract before our department meeting, they would not have been blindsided by his outburst.

I also learned to think carefully about how and when I present information to senior leaders like the executive director. In retrospect, I realized that there is a time and a place to share potentially sensitive information with emotional leaders; discussing the most recent contract negotiation developments as we walked into the department meeting was clearly not the best timing.

Last, I learned to always be up-front and honest with my staff about the actions of senior leadership. While most senior leaders are consummate professionals, they have weaknesses just like the rest of us. Being open and honest about the executive director's emotional tendencies removed the sting from many subsequent encounters my team had with him because they no longer took his responses personally.

Adopting these leadership behaviors paid dividends for my department. Our employee turnover rate decreased substantially, and even the executive director came to realize how his actions affected his colleagues and employees. In the end, the contract—and several others—came through, and my team helped build years of work for our department.

More to Think About and Try

- You are responsible for the leadership of your team and your behaviors set the tone for how your team handles issues.
- Think about how and when you share information with others. Maintain your employees' best interests by keeping them appropriately informed about issues

> involving them. Also, think carefully about how and
> when you share information with senior leaders,
> considering the implications for your employees.
> * Recognize that senior leaders can have shortcomings.
>   How you, as a supervisor, deal with those shortcomings
>   will have a direct impact on your employees.

SUPERVISOR AS ENERGIZER

Supervisors are the energizers-in-chief for their employees. Granted, employees are expected to show up motivated to work. Yet, the way in which a supervisor intentionally energizes his or her employees has a significant impact on the success of those employees as well as the organization. Employee engagement creates a "win" for the employees because they are actively involved in their work, a "win" for the supervisor because he or she is getting the best performance from employees, and a "win" for the organization because it has happy employees who are adding value.

As a supervisor, I recognize that not everyone is motivated by the same things that I am; I try to understand what uniquely energizes each of my direct reports. For example, one of my employees is interested in helping teams work together more effectively and achieve better results. In particular, he likes to help teams of people start to build the trust needed to hold difficult conversations. After working with a team to help them build this type of trust, he will facilitate a series of conversations and team-building activities to get them working more effectively together.

As the supervisor of our work team, I see most of the requests that come in to our team for help. When we get a request for a facilitator to work with a group that is struggling, I assess whether this is a good fit for my employee. Sometimes it is, and sometimes it isn't. The thing that is important is that I am *intentionally* on the lookout for opportunities that will energize him. Whenever possible, I put him in those situations. While he must motivate himself before walking into the room to work with the group, as his supervisor I can provide him opportunities that are energizing. We check in with each other a few times a year to see if he is still energized by this type of work.

A supervisor acting as energizer-in-chief understands every member of the team and finds ways to understand what motivates and energizes them. The best supervisors are always scanning the work environment for opportunities that will be exciting and engaging for their employees. Supervisors who find ways to energize their employees will be rewarded with happier employees, fewer complaints, stronger relationships, enhanced performance, increased contributions, and better results on every level.

More to Think About and Try

- **Get to know what motivates and engages your employees.** Take the time to ask them about times in their careers when they were most (and least) energized and engaged. What can you replicate (or avoid) to help energize your employees?
- **Intentionally seek opportunities to put people in motivating situations.** As a supervisor you are responsible for setting performance plans, making work assignments, and delegating work. Look for assignments and organizational opportunities (certain project teams, for example) that will provide participants a chance to engage.

> • ***Conduct semiannual meetings to check in on team members' energy levels.*** Use the meeting to focus on times over the past six months when the individuals were engaged or not. Determine what actions you can take over the next six months to energize each employee and foster greater engagement.

SUPERVISOR AS COACH

Coaching has arrived in the workplace for a simple reason: done correctly, it works—not only to improve performance but also to strengthen relationships, build future capacity, and help individuals grow beyond their expectations.

My first experience with coaching was as a receiver of coaching from my supervisor. Now as an executive and leadership coach, I still find myself calling on what I learned through this first supervisory coaching experience.

People hold wildly differing concepts of coaching. One person may remember a great sports coach from 8th grade. Another may think of a wise, seasoned mentor. Some people think of coaching as something you punitively do to someone who has not performed. A definition of coaching I like to use is: *a series of question-based conversations in which the supervisor helps the employee gain new insights that translate into action and learning, thereby creating a higher level of performance.*

A conversation is not an order or a demand. A conversation is two-way. In a coaching conversation, the coach mainly listens and asks questions. The assumption in the coaching relationship is that the employee will create and own the solution. The supervisor's questions should be designed to help the employee explore his or her own thinking, assumptions, and frames of reference—the way he or she looks at things. It is a bit like changing the person's "operating system." Once an employee relinquishes old constraints, flawed assumptions, limits, and erroneous filters, options and choices start to expand.

Here are some questions you can use to help an employee expand his or her frame of reference:

- What is another way of viewing this situation you are in?
- What are your assumptions? What would happen if any of those changed?
- Is there anything you are overlooking?
- What have you previously learned about this kind of situation?
- What are some possibilities for new, next steps?
- What do you feel you need to make progress on this situation?

Rely on your intuition as a supervisor to generate these kinds of questions. Listen to your employee and listen to your own instincts as well. The more effective the questions are, the greater the likelihood that both parties will be able to relax into their roles and tap into all their resources.

Because coaching is a distinct role, the supervisor and employee must be clear when they are entering a coaching conversation. The starting point is permission to coach. The supervisor must obtain this permission before starting, and clearly demarcate where the coaching starts and stops.

Another key in a coaching situation is insight. An insight is a cognitive or emotional pivot point—a point of departure or potential change. An insight might be to finally "get" how someone else sees a situation. It could be realizing that an assumption is limiting progress. ("I could never do that.") Often, an insight is about how your own thinking has been steering you away from an effective outcome. It could also be a fundamentally different way to perceive a problematic situation. Many times, employees become aware of how emotions—particularly anger, frustration, stress, and futility—have shaped and misshaped their thinking.

Insight in and of itself has little value; it must be coupled with action. Part of your supervisory coaching role is to help your employees create accountabilities for acting on their new knowledge or awareness. Goal setting, milestones, and a clear sense of the destination are all part of harvesting the insight into something useful.

More to Think About and Try

- Coaching between a supervisor and employee aims to achieve a tangible goal and assumes a dynamic state, simply because two humans are involved. If you ever find yourself confused or unsure about the direction or intent of coaching, the easiest way to stay grounded is to view it as a conversation in which you are helping someone get to a goal, primarily by asking questions that will unlock new possibilities.
- Coaching is one of the most powerful high-performance levers available to any supervisor to learn from and grow—and at the same time create a gift of potentially incalculable value to an employee.

SUPERVISOR AS FACILITATOR

You're a new supervisor about to meet with your direct reports for the first staff meeting. The reason for the new team is a reorganization to streamline processes, talent, and resources. You've been with the group for three weeks and have met with everyone individually to introduce yourself and get to know them and what they do. You've called a staff meeting to gather ideas for developing a new process for working with an important customer. Half of the team members have worked with this customer for ten years. The remaining members are newly hired high-potential employees and transfers from other agencies who have a wide scope of experience but have not worked with this customer. You see a blend of experience, skills, talent, and personalities on your team.

To start the meeting you introduce comments from the customer that the team is taking too long to get back to them. Your goal for the meeting is to solicit feedback from your team on the possible causes for the delay and potential solutions to meet the customer's expectations for improved service.

You open the meeting explaining why you have brought the team together and ask them for their ideas. The team sits in silence; clearly they don't feel comfortable with you or the group yet. How do you get them to engage and offer their insights on potential solutions?

After a few awkward minutes, you pose a question to the group to see if it will get them involved: "What could we do to improve our relationship with this customer?" Silence. You pick someone from the group and ask him a direct question; you get a brief response. More silence. This is how the meeting goes for the next ten minutes. Then, someone in the group decides to offer a controversial solution that would conflict with processes used for other customers of similar size and importance. All of a sudden the group comes to life; the passion for and against the idea is visceral and the silent awkwardness gives way to yelling and interrupting. Members of your team are leaning forward and trying to speak over others who want to get their objections out and impose their own solutions. Now what do you do?

As a supervisor you will be responsible for facilitating hundreds of meetings in the course of your career. You have to know how to pull people out of their silence as well as how to quiet down over-enthusiastic contributors. Facilitating is about encouraging contributions and guiding the voices to meet your objectives. A skilled facilitator knows how to prepare ahead of time to manage the energy in the room no matter how low or high it gets.

Facilitation is a critical skill for every supervisor to master. Supervisors find themselves facilitating frequently to check the pulse of their team in terms of performance, strategic initiatives, feedback, and ideas. A supervisor needs to know how to flush out the nuggets of information and distinguish what is important. It is also important to know when to shut down the noise and guide the group in another direction to meet the objective of the gathering. Whenever people are assembled and dialogue is being shared to express individual points of view, there will always be a need for a supervisor to practice skillful facilitation.

More to Think About and Try

- As a supervisor, your role as a facilitator is to ensure that the conversation remains aligned with the agreed-upon objectives and direction of the group. By establishing the purpose of the gathering and group communication norms, you will be creating the map that you and your team will use to reach the desired outcome.
- Work to maintain balance in who speaks during a meeting. Pull people out of their heads with open-ended, thought-provoking questions and then manage the flow of responses. Learn to quiet the loud voices in the room by using techniques to maintain control, such as asking a question to bring others into the conversation.
- To conclude a session you facilitate, know where you are with time and always recap the points made during the discussion. It is good practice to check with each person on the team at the end of the meeting for final thoughts and last-minute contributions.

■ SUPERVISOR AS MENTOR

Supervising other supervisors who have great expertise and experience in how their work is done can make your job easier... until there is a change. For example, when a subordinate supervisor decides to leave the organization, you may be left to step into that supervisor role on a temporary basis. There are many ways to approach this situation. I learned early on to use the opportunity to be a "temp" supervisor to learn more about the work and people I ultimately have responsibility for—and to mentor others in achieving our goals.

I was appointed director of an organization that provided support services to customers. A critical part of the work involved developing frequent and numerous detailed estimates of the cost of services in response to customer requests. This responsibility was carried out by a team led by a supervisor who reported to me. The supervisor had long experience with the program, was very knowledgeable, and had great rapport with our customers. There was no reason to question the effectiveness of the operation. Response time was typically 72 hours or less, there were few customer complaints, and staff morale appeared to be good. Satisfied with the operation, I was able focus on other program areas and responsibilities that needed my direct attention.

After I had been director several months, my subordinate supervisor accepted another job. That meant that I needed a crash course on the details of daily operations so I could supervise and mentor the work of the team until I could hire a replacement. In addition to discussions with the departing supervisor, I reached out to the staff and customers to gain their perspectives. That's how I learned what was really happening:

- Responsibility for preparing the cost estimates had been completely controlled by the supervisor. Staff members provided input as needed, but the supervisor personally prepared and delivered all estimates.
- None of the staff members had a full understanding of the operation. Each performed a specific set of duties that contributed to the final product, but was unaware of how the pieces came together and how the final product was produced. The staff members felt that they were not trusted to make decisions.
- Customers were tolerant of a 72-hour turnaround time standard but were sometimes frustrated with it. They thought we could do better. While they had a good relationship with the departing supervisor, they were bothered by their complete dependency on the availability of a single employee to prepare estimates.

The process of preparing estimates required collecting prescribed information, paying close attention to detail, formatting properly, and following certain rules. There was no reason why most of the staff could not be trained to do this work. I identified a mid-level staffer who, with mentoring and support, learned the process and in turn taught others. They were all excited to learn this skill. Through this process we encouraged the staff to make decisions and to take accountability for them. We also adopted a general rule that mistakes are allowed but should not be concealed or repeated. Placing trust in the team members gave them confidence, and few mistakes were made.

As we gradually increased the number of staff members empowered to submit estimates, the team talked among themselves and with the customers and reached agreement on a new time standard: We would provide quotes within 24 hours of receiving requests. Staff challenged each other—and supported each other—to meet the more demanding standard and customer satisfaction improved dramatically.

Finally, I helped prepare the staff to participate in the selection of their new supervisor. Together we developed a list of questions for the group interviews with the final candidates. We all agreed that we wanted a strong supervisor who would ensure accountability for the work to be done—and who would also guide and mentor each member of the team to produce high-quality and timely work.

More to Think About and Try

- The appearance of control can be misleading. Employees and customers are often reluctant to share their true feelings about how well an operation is working, even when they know there is room for improvement. Yet, most people want to be—and get excited about being—involved in making decisions that improve results within their organizations. As a supervisor, you can mentor others by involving them in specific skill-building activities.

- When you take the opportunity to share your expertise and experiences with others, you are assuming the role of a mentor. Mentoring can occur one-on-one or in groups.

- Mentoring can work equally well in face-to-face situations or when your team members are located in different places. Establishing clear communication channels and being able to sense your connection with others will make your mentoring opportunities more productive and satisfying.

SUPERVISOR AS PLANNER

As a supervisor, you will be called on to create plans to move your team or organization forward. Planning involves being prepared for many eventualities, including events beyond your control. You never know when you will have to adjust your course in response to rapidly changing circumstances, while maintaining momentum and keeping your employees' focus and commitment strong.

I was responsible for a team of six internal employees as well as two external vendors who were charged with creating a project plan and communications strategy for a five-day global event for new managers. The scope and complexity of the program were overwhelming. The plan was to fly 500 international employees to a large corporate resort. Every moment of each day was to be filled with learning new skills as well as networking opportunities.

Although I had planned and delivered programs for senior-level executives before, the budget, resources, and time allotted to this program were far beyond what had been allotted for any other program. As I assumed my new role, my chief learning officer left the firm. His replacement, the new director, had a different style. She would yell and blame employees for mistakes, no matter how minor. Morale was dropping rapidly due to the organization's unstable financial circumstances as well as the new director's short fuse.

My team was particularly concerned about the success of this program, given the style of the new director. As a result, I first shared my vision of success, the planning process we would follow, and expectations of each staff role. The two key themes of my message were: (1) if something goes wrong, we will solve it and move on, and (2) we need to trust each other.

The next step I took was to leverage knowledge from prior mistakes and successes. I looked through evaluations of previous events to find out what had worked and what had not. Some insights were predictable and some surfaced new learning. One thing I noted was that during every event a few participants would experience miscellaneous problems, such as flight scheduling, family illness, or unfamiliarity with host country customs. This insight prompted me to assign a team member to act as an onsite ombudsman; if, on day one, a participant needed emergency dental care, we would be right on it.

A week before our event, the CEO—who was supposed to be our opening day keynote speaker—was fired. To top it off, the hotel staff where the event was to be held went on strike. This meant we had to expect loud, noisy picketers and no room service for participants who arrived after hours.

Knowing that I had a detailed project plan and flow of the show already prepared, I was able to act quickly to secure the acting CEO to fill in for the keynote. In response to the strike, we purchased bags and filled them with bottled water and treats. My team knew the plan was always available so that responsibility could be delegated and success would be shared. Constant communication was critical.

Although I assumed management of the plan and flow of the show, my team knew this was "our" event. They took ownership to heart, adapted to the continuous changes, and delivered the most successful learning event to date. It was gratifying to watch my team enjoy applause from appreciative participants on the last night of the event.

This experience taught me a lot about the role of a supervisor as a planner:

- The ability to plan is critical to leading employees; this skill continues to improve with experience.
- My team relied on my ability to keep adapting, calmly, in the midst of change. The plan supported that calm demeanor.
- Good planning involves building upon and leveraging prior lessons and experiences.
- A well-laid-out planning process can be a rudder through either stable or rapidly changing conditions.
- A plan can be an effective communication tool that permits information-sharing versus information-hoarding.
- Planning transparency builds in accountability. Individuals will demonstrate greater diligence in contributing deliverables on time.
- Planning enables task delegation versus micro-management.
- A good plan can be an effective tool for moving past or around obstacles to achieve a successful outcome.

More to Think About and Try

- Planning involves moving the process forward, while being prepared for events to change.
- A solid plan enables delegation of responsibility and collective ownership of the goal.
- In chaotic external environments, it is critical to focus on the plan as your communication and accountability roadmap for everyone to use.

SUPERVISOR AS CONSULTANT

A consultant is often hired by leaders and work groups to give them "expert advice" on how to solve their performance or personnel problems. A successful consultant builds long-term relationships with the customer.

A supervisor can also function as a consultant, helping the people she leads solve performance or personnel problems. This can begin as a front-line supervisor and continue as you move up to new levels of supervision. As you rise in the organization and continue to solve bigger problems, along the way you build stronger relationships with people across the entire organization.

Sheila has just been promoted to manage a small, six-person customer service department that handles network help requests for the regional office of an agency. The department's objectives are to assess the problem and then either solve the problem or refer it to a systems engineer. The department follows up to ensure customer satisfaction; if necessary, the staff reworks the problem until it is resolved.

Sheila is excited to take on her new responsibilities. She has worked with all the team members except one and believes they are all technically competent and capable of doing the job. However, she knows they are not being effective because the recent customer satisfaction survey showed only an 87 percent satisfaction ratio.

Everybody essentially does the same work and except for Marco, everyone is fully trained on using the system and resolving basic network problems. Sheila reflects on her team and their operational processes. She determines that an excellent first step in developing team cohesion and focus is to create "smart" goals (**s**pecific, **m**easurable, **a**greed-upon, **r**easonable, **t**ime-bound) to track across the team. After a series of meetings, the team agrees on the following individual smart goals, which will be reported on a weekly basis:

- **Requests per day:** Each team member should handle on average no less than 15 percent of daily requests. Even if a team member gets more complex requests that affect his or her share on a daily basis, the percentage should average out over the month.
- **Percentage of reworks:** After reviewing some history, the team agrees that less than 5 percent of their requests should be reworks.
- **Customer satisfaction:** Everyone agrees that they should be above a 95 percent satisfaction ratio.

At the end of the first month, signs of trouble within the team are evident.

Based on these measurable results, it is obvious to Sheila that improvements are needed. In addition, Tonya and Beth are making comments about having to do all the work. Li looks lost and Marco almost cries one day. Peggy and Sal constantly grumble about how difficult the work is and how the new reporting is a pain. Sheila moans to herself, "I thought the smart goals would motivate everyone to top performance. What did I miss?"

	Percentage of Requests per Day	Percentage of Reworks	Customer Satisfaction
Tonya	32	4	97
Beth	28	3	98
Li	15	5	92
Marco	10	7	90
Peggy	8	12	85
Sal	7	8	88

Sheila decides to work with everyone individually on performance plans. For Tonya and Beth, she applauds their hard work and rewards their efforts with some extra time off. Sheila asks both of them if they will help her coach the others to bring them up to speed. She sits with Li and Marco separately to assess where they need some coaching or training. Finally, Sheila meets separately with Peggy and Sal. Peggy complains that she feels like she got all of the hardest requests this month, many of which had to be referred and were still not resolved. Sheila reviews the call logs and analyzes each call. She finds that many of the requests were problematic and unusual. She decides to monitor the degree of difficulty of all requests more closely and also to provide some training for Peggy.

Peggy seems to be interested in doing better and is genuinely excited about the extra training. Sal, on the other hand, just complains about the extra reporting taking up time and the customers being ignorant. Sheila senses a lack of motivation and tells Sal that she is initiating a performance improvement work plan for him. Through close supervision and monitoring of his daily activity, Sheila hopes to correct Sal's performance weaknesses and develop a level of trust to ensure he functions independently.

At the end of the second month the smart goals results reflect some positive changes.

	Percentage of Requests per Day	Percentage of Reworks	Customer Satisfaction
Tonya	23	3	97
Beth	20	3	98
Li	17	5	95
Marco	16	7	93
Peggy	12	5	92
Sal	10	4	88

Sheila sees positive changes across the board. Importantly, the complaining is nonexistent. Sheila knows she needs to monitor performance constantly. She is also working on redefining the smart goals around the difficulty of the requests, which will require a process for monitoring and allocating requests based on degree of difficulty.

More to Think About and Try

- When taking a consultative approach, an effective supervisor is able to analyze the problem without blame or judgment. A good way to build this skill is to get into the habit of answering some key questions:
  - What outcome do I really want to achieve?
  - Have I chosen the first solution or the best solution? Are there other alternatives?
  - Have I listened to my team's thoughts on the issue?
  - How can I get the team or individual to partner with me in the outcomes or results?
  - What is the plan for the team or individual?

- As a supervisor, when you are playing the role of consultant it is important to be deliberate and decisive about the outcome you are seeking. Then choose the best methods to achieve that outcome.

SUPERVISOR AS EDUCATOR

I joined the Marine Corps during a difficult time. Just after the Viet Nam War ended in the mid 1970s, I was a supply officer in a unit where most of the troops were barely literate. My experience was that if I didn't do something myself, it just wouldn't get done. To survive, I adapted to the situation by doing all the major tasks myself and carefully monitoring the less important ones assigned to others. The outcome was good—we met all our mission requirements—but I did almost all the work myself; it was tiring and not much fun.

Fast forward two and a half years and I'm in Okinawa in a new engineer battalion that was formed to transfer equipment and personnel from around the regiment. Most of the equipment we received had a yellow "H" spray-painted on it; in the Marine Corps, an "H" means this piece of equipment should be sent to disposal. Almost none of the equipment was actually operable. It was a nightmare.

Here I was, understaffed, and the Marines I did have were not very knowledgeable. The Marine Corps had just implemented new supply and maintenance systems that were a puzzle to most of us in the field. To make matters worse, our new organization's funding was very limited. So, I did what I had always done: I buckled down, educated myself on the new systems, and prepared for another miserable and tiring year.

One day my two staff sergeants came to see me. "Lieutenant," they said, "let us take you to lunch and talk." I was leery at first. One sergeant was very new to supply and the other had not displayed much leadership or ability. But, I went to lunch. It turned out to be a turning point in my career. Their message was twofold: "We want to help, and we need you to teach us what you know."

Over the next few weeks I did just that. Bit by bit, I turned the things I had been doing myself over to them—and we learned together. They were like sponges, soaking up all I threw at them. After a couple of months, I actually started having fun. I could focus on more long-range issues and be a supporter rather than a doer. The two staff sergeants passed what they learned on to others, and soon we had our equipment up and running with a very tight team of supply and maintenance folks. It was a proud day when our unit became fully mission-capable a few weeks before I rotated back to the states.

I learned my lesson and have used this experience in every new supervisory role I have accepted. Throughout my career I have encouraged others to further their education, complete their college degrees, or take skill-building courses. As I advanced, I ensured that my direct reports did the same for those they supervised. We all reaped the benefits.

More to Think About and Try

- Since that early experience in the Marine Corps, training and educating those I work with has become part of my supervisory style. I believe it builds confidence in others while improving their capability and, by extension, enhancing the organization. Specifically:

  - Delegation becomes less risky and allows supervisors to focus their efforts on resolving problems and planning ahead.
  - Succession planning becomes more effective; as you move up, someone is ready to take your place.
  - Making education and training a priority decreases personnel turnover, encourages people to advance, and inspires employees to increase their knowledge.

- As a supervisor, you may worry that when a staff member moves on, you will lose what you have invested—but that won't be the case if training and education are your focus. You will find a line of eager, highly capable candidates ready to take the job as the person leaving spreads the word about what a great boss you are. And, you'll have a lot more fun in your role as a supervisor!

SUPERVISOR AS PUBLIC SERVANT

When I was in the Peace Corps, I learned the importance of paying attention, connecting the dots, being responsive to our hosts, and keeping the mission of the Corps front and center. When I took my first job with a federal agency several years later (organizing community action programs in Appalachia), I had the good fortune of a stellar supervisor who respected my intelligence, was disinclined to micro-manage, and willingly identified technical skills that would make me a more effective supervisor serving the public.

But my role—like that of many supervisory jobs in the federal government—was not straightforward. Our mission seemed vague and complex to me, especially given my front-line role "representing" the government with state and local officials, community groups and leaders, the media, other public interest groups, and stakeholders. Fortunately, my supervisor took time out to coach me and recommend appropriate formal training.

I learned early on that supervisors in the public sector must learn to prepare their direct reports for a more "balanced scorecard" of results than the single, financial bottom line more common in the private sector. In the federal government, interfaces with the public and with other internal and external stakeholders are paramount. As a federal supervisor, you often represent what your agency and program stand for. That's a broader and a deeper responsibility than what a new supervisor would face in the private sector.

When I moved to my first federal agency from the Peace Corps, I received two gifts from my supervisor: (1) technical feedback that enabled me to be a more effective representative of the agency and (2) exposure to the highest levels at the department and other stakeholders in OMB, the White House, and Congress that prepared me for greater responsibility. My supervisor's advice on dealing with the media eventually prepared me to respond effectively to a blogger, a member of the press corps, or a stakeholder in a different agency when they put me on the spot.

Later, reflecting on the public service aspect of supervising in government organizations, I discovered the importance of our agency's mission in motivating executives, managers, and subordinates. More than being able to work effectively and efficiently within our budget, employees were motivated by being part of a more balanced set of outcomes that included stewardship and oversight responsibilities, customer and public satisfaction, and measurable performance results expected by the administration and Congress.

Much of my supervisory effort was directed at reminding our workforce why—and how—our organization was important to achieving these missions, the urgency of implementing our strategies, and how each of us—at whatever level and in whatever capacity—had the opportunity to make a measurable impact on results. Connecting these dots helped motivate others and foster collaboration in our agency and across other government organizations.

More to Think About and Try

- Engage the workforce you supervise as dynamically as possible around the organization's mission. Your team is your most critical resource. Without their full empowerment and commitment, your organization will be handicapped in achieving its purpose.
- Give your team the support and information they need to be successful in serving the public: clear and continuous direction, tools, skills training, and regular feedback.

- Update the workforce on the organization's progress and outcomes, linking back to their measurable contributions as a team. Ask for their input on opportunities to improve their service to show support for the organization's mission.
- While maintaining a focus on strategic mission, invest regularly in the development of individual employees as professional public supervisors, particularly young professionals; they are the government's future.
- Personally model these values in all your dealings with the workforce and with others up and down the chain of command, particularly with external stakeholders and the public.

BLENDING SUPERVISORY ROLES TOGETHER IN A UNIQUE WAY

Each key supervisor role can serve as an energy source for others' performance. In some cases, you will find that a single role is sufficient to address a particular situation. Other times, you may need to blend roles in a unique way to work through the complexities of the situation.

As you acquire new and different experiences as a supervisor, you will naturally strengthen how you perform each supervisory role and increase your comfort in blending different roles when the situation calls for it. The power in supervisory work comes when you connect the needs of those you support with your knowledge, skills, and insights about the situation. Here are a few things to think about when blending the different roles of a supervisor:

- The presenting situation—the problem, issue, or opportunity—is your starting point. As you work through each situation, the roles you need to play will begin to come clear.

- Very often as you get deeper into discussions about a particular situation, you will uncover new and different information. You may need to step in and out of different roles as you redefine the specific situation you will address. Getting clear about the real situation to which you will apply your supervisory knowledge, skills, and insights will allow you to progress toward a solution more easily.

- Taking time to reflect on how things are going while you are working though a supervisory situation will give you the space to make interim adjustments in how you apply and blend different roles. Your continuous learning will help you apply the various supervisory roles as needed when new situations arise.

Whether you are in the early days of supervising someone, working through a problem, building new capacity, or supporting performance improvement, you will have a great impact on others if you learn how to uniquely blend the power of each supervisor role to meet the needs of the situation at hand.

4

Getting the Best Work from Others

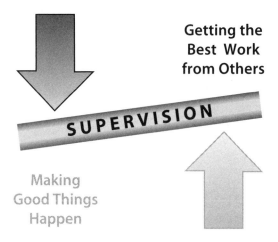

When you decide to take on the many roles of a supervisor, you are deciding to make the shift from being an expert to using your brainpower and experience to access and multiply the potential of others . . . to get things done. This is the essence of supervision.

As a supervisor, your greatest success will come when you personalize how you get the best work from others to make good things happen. First and foremost, this means understanding yourself. However, it also means letting go of being the center of attention. It means investing your time and effort to learn, practice, and be open to many different experiences. It means knowing how to tap into the initiative and imagination of others. It means being able to help others continually grow and develop in new and different ways. It means looking ahead to what is needed, adding value where it matters, and giving your employees space to get real work done.

The first three chapters provided the basics to help ground you in what it means to be a supervisor. Chapters 4 and 5 take you a step further by introducing you to the two key dimensions of supervision: (1) getting the best work from others and (2) making good things happen. Your challenge every day as a supervisor is to keep a balance between getting the best work from others and achieving real work in support of your government organization's mission and goals.

The collection of stories in Chapter 4 is about how supervisors influence human behavior one conversation or action at a time to get the best work from others. Think of this dimension as the people side of supervision.

WHAT HAPPENS WHEN YOU PLACE YOURSELF AT THE CENTER OF ALL DECISIONS?

As the boss, placing yourself at the center of all decisions can seem to make sense. Most important, it keeps you in the loop. After all, you are ultimately responsible for your employees and the work they do. As a supervisor, you have a broader perspective than your employees do, which often helps you make more informed decisions.

Yet there are potential drawbacks: You can become a bottleneck, you are sending a message to your employees that they are not capable of making good decisions, and resources can be wasted as employees wait for you to make a decision and then inform them of it. This story is about a supervisor who insisted that all decisions go through her.

Linda was a GS-15 supervisory IT specialist with more than 20 years of experience working for both the federal government and private sector organizations. She transferred to her current agency to spearhead the installation of a new IT system. Her responsibility was to lead a team of programmers to customize the system and install it on the server. Once the system went online, the team was scheduled to undertake similar system installation projects for other parts of the agency.

Linda's experience made her a good choice for this role—and it showed at the kickoff meeting she held with the team of 12 programmers assigned to her. She took charge of the meeting, presented a project schedule, assigned tasks to the programmers, and instituted daily status meetings. In addition to making all decisions about the modules and system programming, she required that requests for vacation and training go through her.

The team got off to a fast start thanks to Linda's strong command. After a couple of months, one of the programmers, Lee, decided to make some improvements to the code that he had been assigned to work on. He had always been a top performer, and his previous bosses had nominated him for several recognition awards based on his ability to make systems run faster with fewer glitches. At the daily status meeting, Lee indicated that he had completed his module. Several days later when she was performing a quality check, Linda realized that Lee had tackled the code in a different way than she had originally outlined.

At the daily meeting, Linda reprimanded Lee, ordering him to immediately reprogram the module according to her plan. Jerry, who was integrating Lee's module into his own assignments, tried to explain how Lee had improved processing speed threefold and how his approach could improve several other modules. Linda snapped Jerry back in line quickly.

Linda's response was the first of many times she reined in the team's initiative. She felt she had no choice but to assert her authority and make sure they made no decisions on their own. The team became more and more frustrated and confused. They thought they had proven themselves to Linda as highly capable programmers and should be allowed to take initiative in changing the design if it improved the system.

Progress began to slow. The team spent more and more time venting to each other about Linda's unwillingness to give up any decision-making authority. Because she was reviewing each line of code herself, she had little time to carry out her administrative duties. One team member signed up to attend a day-long training session but couldn't go because Linda hadn't approved the request in time.

When Linda took a bad fall down her stairs at home, she had to have back surgery and was out of the office for several months. Although any of the team's 12 members could have stepped in to run the project, no one was willing to do so. They were afraid of making a decision that Linda would not agree with when she returned. The project did not complete on time and the team members eventually moved on to other agency IT projects.

More to Think About and Try

- Consider delegating decision-making authority when you are undertaking a long-term project or assignment and when employees have enough information to make informed decisions. When you have a cohesive work group, you will be able to delegate decision-making and feel confident the team will share and accept the decisions. Giving others a chance to hone their decision-making skills will help you grow a team and develop your employees' professional skills.

- When you delegate decision-making authority, be sure to communicate clearly the types of decisions you are delegating, along with the responsibility not only to make a good decision but also to share the decision with you and others who are impacted by it.

- Empower your team members to make informed decisions that are likely to have favorable outcomes. Your employees may come up with new ideas that you never thought of—then they look good and you look good!

MAKING CHOICES

Throughout the years as a supervisor I have had many opportunities to make choices. The area that has helped me learn the most about making good choices is the process of hiring new employees. I have built business cases and position justifications. I have written position descriptions and recruitment postings. After HR collected the qualified resumes, as the hiring manager, I have selected the individuals I wanted to interview. I have conducted interviews and made hiring decisions.

Each organization had its own customized, but hardly unique, process. Anyone who hires for the government knows that it is an involved process. There are layers of checkpoints required to hire a new employee: KSAs are aligned, resumes are cross-referenced, references are checked, and numerous interviews are conducted.

One of the most valuable lessons I learned about making choices was as a young supervisor at an Army facility overseas. Following all the normal hiring process steps, I had narrowed the pool down to two qualified but very different candidates.

The first candidate was an experienced employee who had held several jobs within the military community. Her technical skills for the specific job were acceptable; however, her knowledge of the government/military culture was extensive. The second candidate had just finished college and possessed a high level of technical skills for the job but had no knowledge of the intricate workings of military or government processes. As I talked with my boss about the best person for the job, we were both perplexed about which candidate to hire; both seemed to be good fits for the job. In the end, we decided it would be easier to work with someone familiar with government/military culture even though her technical skills were not as strong. We hired the first candidate.

The decision was based upon our wanting someone who could "hit the ground running," and I had rationalized that it would be easier for me as her supervisor to fill in the technical gaps than to train her on government processes and culture.

Unfortunately, the first candidate turned out to be the nightmare employee. Even though she had been properly vetted through the government hiring process, I quickly discovered the reason she had worked at so many places: her poor work ethic. Moreover, she was unable to demonstrate the depth of technical skills she had stated on her resume. It can be difficult to fire an employee, and I learned that most of her former employers had taken the road of making the workplace intolerable so she would leave on her own.

By law, former employers are not allowed to disclose much information about employees and people tend to be especially reluctant to talk about a bad employee. In the end, this employee consumed excessive amounts of my time and the whole department suffered. She ended up being fired for simply not coming to work. We subsequently hired the second candidate, who worked successfully for our organization for years.

More to Think About and Try

- You will make many choices each day; some will be easier than others. Always start by understanding the specific situation you are in that requires you to make a choice.
- Abide by any processes that will help guide you in making the right choice. However, be aware that even if you use a thorough process, there is no guarantee that the choice you make will net the result you are seeking. For example, in the case of hiring, candidate references often do not provide a complete picture.
- Get input from others to help you fully understand the options before making a choice.
- Be clear about why you are making the specific choice and be able to state any assumptions you have about the choice.
- When a choice involves people, pay attention to their verbal and non-verbal communication. You will come away with insights that will help you make a better choice.
- Take the risk on an unknown if it feels right. Listen to your intuition. If you have an uneasy gut feeling about a choice, explore what's behind it.
- Once you make a choice, remember to take the time to reflect on it and learn for next time.

RESOLVING TEAM CONFLICT TOGETHER

Recognizing and addressing conflict instead of avoiding it are crucial to the success of any team. Those words are easy to say, but not always easy to act upon.

Often there are clues. For me, I came to the realization that I was avoiding conflict on my team when communication between my team members began to occur only when necessary. Specifically, when I discovered that my team members were using other forms of communication (like email) to avoid personal interaction, I realized I needed to address the situation.

The conflict among members of my team was manifesting itself in some significant ways. The work environment had become negative and some pretty thick walls had developed between the team members, both personally and professionally. While the team managed their day-to-day work well and kept our customers happy, we were not performing as a team on a fundamental level. We were a team in turmoil.

As a supervisor, I considered a couple of ways I could address the team conflict. I could talk with each individual separately. Or, I could address the conflict as a team, playing the role of moderator. Neither of these options seemed just right. So after careful thought and consideration, I came up with a third option that I thought would serve our team better. Since I was a part of this team, not an outsider looking in, I needed to be a part of resolving the conflict—as a team member rather than a moderator.

I took this idea to my supervisor and we talked over the idea of bringing in a team coach. She was very supportive of the idea. Over a period of three months, the team coach engaged us in several working sessions. We learned about our individual communication style preferences, as well as our similarities and differences. We also learned more about each other on a personal level. Through this process, we began to understand each other as unique individuals. We also developed an appreciation for our individual contributions to the team, to the larger divisional team, and to our overall organization.

Through these working sessions, we created a foundation of respect and trust with each other. To ensure we continued to make progress, we agreed on actions we would each take to communicate and work together as a team. The team continued to make efforts to enhance the level of trust that had been established. Through regular team meetings, our communication with each other continued to get stronger. The team also committed to participate in periodic team-building activities throughout the rest of the year. We met this goal and our ability to deal with conflict improved significantly.

Others who worked with and around us noticed the changes and commented not only on the personal changes they observed, but also on the enhanced customer service we were providing to our colleagues and customers.

More to Think About and Try

- Recognizing, as a supervising team leader, that you are part of a team is an important aspect of addressing team conflict.
- When a team works through challenges together, it can be source of pride for all.
- Seeking outside expertise to help a team work through conflict can speed the process of behavior change.

- Ongoing reflection, assessment, and learning are important to ensure the team continues to grow and perform.
- Addressing conflict yields benefits for each individual team member as well as the larger organization and the customers it serves.

FINDING COMMON GROUND

During a recent visit to my local Department of Motor Vehicles, I found the staff person I was dealing with to be absolutely irascible. I needed a new parking placard for my car because my current one had been stolen. After about five minutes of going nowhere, I stepped back and looked at the situation, my surroundings, and the person on the other side of the counter. I noticed pictures of dogs under the glass on the service side of the desk. Being a dog lover myself, I jumped at the opportunity to ask the service person about her dogs. She immediately melted, we talked about our dogs, and I got my new placard.

This event has much in common with the day-to-day operations in a helpdesk or a service department. We often have to deal with angry or upset customers, and are always looking for that common ground.

Over the years as a supervisor of a helpdesk and a development staff, I have learned a lot about dealing with a broad spectrum of people. I have dealt with people across all lines and levels of employee and personality. They were facing a wide variety of challenges or situations. Through these experiences, I came up with an easy way to approach difficult people and reach common ground more quickly.

Seek answers to three simple questions:

- *Who?* Knowing as much as possible about the person you are dealing with is important. Try to figure out who this person is—outside the office as well as in the office. Does he have hobbies or interests? You may be able to relate to him by finding out what he does outside his job.
- *What?* Think of the person as a customer. What is it she really wants? Is she able to articulate what is important to her? If not, try to help her.
- *Why?* Does this person have outside pressures you don't know about? Does he have special circumstances you may not be aware of? Is he being asked to do something differently? People operate out of habit; it is difficult for them to change if they don't know any other way. Offer ideas. Suggest ways the individual might achieve his aims more effectively.

As a supervisor, you will undoubtedly have to deal with a difficult or challenging person. If we just take a moment to step back and evaluate the individual, his situation, and the environmental context, you may find him to be less of a challenge and more of an opportunity. Finding common ground then becomes a lot easier.

More to Think About and Try

- *Focus your energy.* Where attention goes, energy flows. What we focus on tends to expand. Energy spent on negativity is energy that could instead be spent on something of greater value. I have found that once I allow negativity into one area of my life, it starts to subtly bleed into other areas as well. We carry that energy with us as we go about our day. When we don't feel good, we lose clarity and even react unconsciously to other areas of our lives.

- **Relish your successes.** If you work though problems successfully and reach common ground, don't forget to celebrate.

I WISH MY BOSS WOULD WALK IN MY SHOES

"My boss does not have a clue what it takes to get things done. If she would walk in my shoes, she would appreciate the challenges I face every day." Have you ever felt that way about a supervisor? As a supervisor, you have many responsibilities and competing interests; nevertheless, it is important not to lose sight of how your decisions impact others.

I have seen supervisors at higher levels in the federal government lose sight of what it takes for those below them to the handle the complexities and scope of their job every day to achieve results. In my current role, I am responsible for coordinating documents that detail and describe my department's overarching policy on how it conducts its mission and many critical business aspects. These documents set clear and consistent organizational approaches for department employees to follow.

On a fairly regular basis, my supervisor tries to circumvent the system and "push" the document coordination process, which can take 8–10 weeks to complete. She invariably wants me to make an exception or change the process because she's received a request to expedite or bypass a critical step in order to move things along faster. As a result, I find myself continuously explaining—and re-explaining—the approved department process for coordinating the documents to my supervisor.

At times I have given in to my supervisor's special requests. Not surprisingly, it is on those occasions that senior executive leadership has not approved the documents. Because my role is to oversee the coordination process, it does not reflect favorably on me when I try to go around the steps I ask others to follow. Besides the blame I receive, deviating from the process creates confusion for many other employees in the department. When they have to step out of the normal process, it takes time to accommodate the changes and to smooth over the issues created by the special requests.

More to Think About and Try

- When you ask someone to make an exception yet still be accountable, you create a dilemma that is difficult to reconcile.
- In any situation, each person brings a different perspective. Being open to others' perspectives will enable you to gain new insights and thereby make better decisions.
- When you take the time to understand the current situation and why things are the way they are, it becomes easier to introduce change that ends up being the right thing to do.
- If you are looking at the immediate situation only, you may inadvertently be creating more difficulties for situations that arise later.

ADDRESSING POOR PERFORMANCE

One of the most difficult aspects of becoming an effective supervisor is telling an employee that he or she is not fulfilling the duties of the position satisfactorily. Yet failing to address inadequate performance creates resentment, perpetuates poor performance, and limits individual and team productivity and growth. I found that I was very comfortable in my supervisory role when it called for me to act as a coach or facilitator. However, I tended to avoid difficult conversations when performance issues arose.

Employees appreciate direct, fact-based conversations that are not clouded with ambiguity. I learned that lesson the hard way.

I joined an organization during a period of change and was assigned a long-heralded employee. Over time, I noticed that her performance was very much rooted in past practices and she was not adhering to new guidelines and policies. When I observed her interacting with the team that she in turn supervised, it became apparent that her lack of follow-through with the new regulations was adversely affecting the performance of her team members. Several casual conversations in which I made friendly "suggestions" had no impact. So, following a specific performance incident, I met with her to review the incident and discuss a proposed formal plan for improvement.

I was nervous. She had a long history with the organization and I was a fresh face and quite a bit younger (she had already pointed out that her son was my age). I opened the conversation with a short summary of what I had observed. I framed each comment in a positive light, even though I was truly displeased with her performance. I then transitioned the conversation to the improvement plan and began to review its contents. She became furious and angrily said she had been "blindsided." I encouraged her to think about our conversation. She responded with a formal and emotionally charged rebuttal to my proposed plan.

I took the time to reflect on the meeting, trying to be as objective as possible. Fortunately, I was enrolled in a supervisory course at the time. I went through my formal course readings, which helped me understand how I could prepare for and approach my next difficult conversation differently.

Only a few months later I found myself in a similar situation. This time, I scripted my entire observation of my employee's interactions with his team and then analyzed the script for patterns. Sure enough, there were numerous examples of the types of issues I had informally noticed over several months. I prepared a formal write-up and an improvement plan, this time including specific examples.

When the employee arrived at my office, I welcomed him, gave him a copy of my written observations, and began reviewing the details with him. I started with a concise summary of the context of my observations. I then specifically addressed three patterns that had emerged, framing my language in a way that stressed the impact of his decisions on his team's performance. I quoted comments he had made that I had documented as specific examples.

At the end of each of the three sections, I paused to allow him time to absorb my comments and respond. When he began to disagree, I went back to the specific examples of unacceptable behavior. I also asked him what support or resources would help him change the behaviors that needed to be addressed. I documented those requests in the improvement plan. As his supervisor, it was my responsibility to facilitate his access to sources of support.

By the end of the meeting, he actually thanked me. I arranged for a job coach to mentor him and provided funding for additional training. His performance improved—as did his team's performance.

More to Think About and Try

- *Clearly define the issue and what needs to change.*
  Be transparent. What does success look like in that
  particular role? Where are the gaps? Which specific
  items need to change immediately and which can evolve
  over time? Once you have fully developed responses to
  these questions, you will be more prepared to turn poor
  performance into effective performance.
- *Let the facts speak.* Documenting specific examples
  of problem areas helps employees see what needs to
  change. Relying on observations, data, and specific
  examples instead of allowing the conversation to become
  a personal judgment creates room for positive growth.
- *Solicit input from the employee—and follow through
  with timely support.* While you as the supervisor may know
  exactly what is missing from the employee's performance,
  you may not be aware of all the factors involved. Allowing
  the employee to have a voice in the support needed will
  encourage ownership of the solution, which will in turn
  make the journey toward effective change easier and more
  successful. Most important, follow through with those
  resources and support in a timely manner.

GIVING AND RECEIVING FEEDBACK

I was terrified—as stressed as I have ever been.

Not only was I scheduled to receive *my* performance evaluation
from my supervisor, but it was the first time in my federal career
to give reviews to my team—six individuals of wildly varying
skills, personalities, competencies, and years of service. I was the

young kid on the block; they were seasoned, and I had to give *them* feedback.

There had been grumbling in the office. The team felt that a lot of previous feedback had been subjective and ungrounded; others said it was one-sided and boss-dominated. Some thought we should do away with performance evaluations entirely. I went to my previous boss—a woman who had been a mentor to me before I was promoted—and asked for advice.

"Sure, some performance reviews can be dysfunctional, but they don't have to be," she said. "Most of the time, performance feedback elicits improved performance. Not only can a review help employees recognize their strengths and developmental needs, but if done well it can boost their motivation."

To my "fresh supervisor" ears, that sounded like a miracle! I asked what I would have to do to get those kinds of results from a feedback session.

"See it as a *conversation* between a supervisor and a subordinate," she suggested. The values of both parties guide conversations so you can explore and express performance concerns and opportunities for development openly.

She went on to offer some additional points:

- **The best time to give feedback is as soon as possible.** The best feedback is not at the end of the year, but in "real time." But be sure to give it when *you* are ready—not emotional or angry. Think about what you need to say, then say it.

- **Feedback is a two-way dialogue, so you can open the session by asking, "What do you think has gone well for you this year?"** Encouraging open communication helps the person receiving the feedback reflect on both past performance and the potential to emerge as a better employee.

- **Feedback works best when it is seen as a way to improve performance.** Objectivity is critical. Focus on facts and concrete events or behaviors. Instead of saying "I think you could be putting in more hours," try something like "I would have liked to see you participate actively in project XYZ, which required supporting the other team for two days last month." Make your point and have specific documentation on hand to support it.

- **Ask the employee what she thinks she could have done better or learned from a difficult situation.** Employees know when they have missed the mark; when they identify their failures, you can discuss areas for personal growth. This question always yields honest self-reflection and commitment to applying the lesson learned.

- **Give constant feedback.** If an employee is not doing well, talk about it immediately. Catching undesirable behaviors early allows you to correct them. Celebrating good performance quickly can provide a motivational boost. The more often a supervisor gives feedback, the easier it becomes.

- **Balance evaluation and development.** Criticism often makes people emotional and upset, even when it is constructive. When emotions are high, it is difficult to keep focus. Give the employee time to collect his or her thoughts. Strive for an open conversation focused on learning and development.

- *"Next steps" can often be the most important part of giving feedback.* It gives you as a supervisor time to state your expectations clearly and set a time frame for accomplishing them. By asking, "What do you want to work on during the next year that will contribute to our goals and mission?" you will move your employee to a higher level of performance.

The first round of performance feedback went well, and I knew I would get better with more experience. I tried to remember that each person I talked with wants to be successful on the job and wants me to be straightforward and committed to his development and contributions.

Some months later I found myself with a new opportunity to test my feedback skills.

One of my employees was not happy with the results of a meeting. She got up during the meeting and stormed off, leaving the other attendees in her wake. This was not the first time she had signaled that she was unhappy with the direction the team was taking. Yet, she had never been confronted with the inappropriateness of her behavior. Clearly, this type of behavior could no longer be ignored.

I sat down with her and described what she—and the entire team—had witnessed. The employee did not try to justify or rationalize her behavior. She acknowledged that it was inappropriate and that she needed to find a more productive way to verbalize her perspectives.

In the past, team members had tried to provide feedback in a multitude of indirect ways. None of these seemed to work. Now, however, the one-on-one feedback session with me focused on the specific behavior and was timely, yielding a positive outcome.

More to Think About and Try

- *Listen.* It is amazing how many sides to a story there are.
- *Create a safe environment for learning.* Help others feel safe to make mistakes and learn from them.
- *Focus on behaviors, not personalities.* Specificity counts—in words, documentation, follow-through, goals, and plans.

ESTABLISHING TRUST AND CONFIDENCE

I was selected to take a supervisory position managing a program with which I had been familiar for many years. I was excited about the opportunity to lead a good group of people and make it better. This was a move from headquarters to a field operation. I knew several of the people who would be reporting to me from work on "headquarters" projects and had as favorable a view of them as I believed they had of me. I thought they would be happy to have someone with central office support and connections. Little did I know that they saw me as a headquarters spy who stole the job from the local guy who had been acting director! In this case the relationships began before initial contact, as most of the team had negative thoughts and feelings before I even reported for duty.

This was a field organization that had achieved success without drawing too much attention to itself. The supervisor role was one I had dreamed of having for a long time. Agency leadership had plans for major changes affecting the program in all the field organizations. I knew it was my job to work through the mandated changes while preserving the many things that had made the program successful for so long. To do this I needed to establish the trust and confidence of the staff quickly.

The job required lots of time away from the office traveling to headquarters, other field locations, and customer sites. At the first opportunity, I called the staff together to report on my upcoming travel plans. I told them that I had the highest respect for their work and would be a strong advocate for them and the program to the central office. I announced that the unsuccessful local candidate would be my deputy (I had talked with him before the meeting) and would have a key leadership role in day-to-day operations as well as full responsibility in "acting" status when I was away from the office. He had the respect of the staff before I arrived and I wanted to show my respect as well.

At this point, what people heard were only words. I needed to back them up with action.

One of our contractors had been seeking a raise in his rate for some time and my deputy, as acting director, had denied it repeatedly. Shortly after my arrival, the contractor asked for a meeting and made his pitch. Increasing the rate was within my authority and there was some merit to his argument, but I felt it was important to reinforce my deputy's stance so I did not agree to the increase.

On my arrival, I observed very quickly that the operation ran smoothly. This was due in large part to the effectiveness of the "office manager," who led the administrative and operational support team. She was knowledgeable, hard-working, and respected by all the staff. I met with her to discuss her role and asked if she would be willing to take on some additional assignments to support me directly. I had reviewed her job description and noted that it did not accurately reflect her job duties. I asked her to update the job description so I could submit it for a promotion. In time her promotion came through, but just recognizing her contributions was sufficient to win her support.

Gradually, I began to make other changes. I knew all along that I was selected in part to bring a new perspective to the program and to balance headquarters interests with field-level realities.

More to Think About and Try

- *Those "in the know" can help you introduce change.* I believe that quick change would have hurt, not strengthened, the program. As much as I thought I knew about the operation and how it could be improved, the people who were there before me knew so much more. They also knew what needed to be improved.
- *Great ideas for improvement often come from within.* By giving visible and meaningful support to two key people, I knew I would get the best ideas for improvement from all the staff. Otherwise I would run the risk of making uninformed decisions. It is also possible that the staff would have found ways to undermine my efforts.
- *Working together builds trust and confidence.* Going forward, the team agreed on many decisions for change and we implemented them vigorously. Where we did not agree, we worked together with mutual respect to get the job done.

I LIKE IT WHEN MY BOSS LAUGHS AT HIMSELF AND HAS FUN

When my boss laughs at himself and has fun, it is contagious; his laughter provokes laughter from others on the team. Laughter helps people feel at ease around each other. If you have ever been the only person in a group who did not get a joke, you probably already know that laughter is critical to successful social interactions.

Let me tell you about my supervisor, Will.

Will somehow finds a way to express his amusement, especially during hectic times. After working long hours on an important project, Will asks his team during an in-person meeting what they learned on the project. After a long, uncomfortable silence, Will answers that we should not have waited until the end of the project to meet at the bar for drinks. His lighthearted response releases the tension in the room, allowing others to comfortably offer their feedback.

When leading his own team meetings, Will often arrives late. His team recognizes his tremendous work effort and sense of humor. Rather than pout, the team takes his cue to openly use humor to defuse conflict by kicking off the meeting with witty remarks: "Will you be on time?" "No," the room roars, "we're on Will-adjusted time." Definitions of Will-adjusted time follow. The team openly responds to Will's humor and directs the joking right back at him.

More to Think About and Try

- Try using humor and laughter with others to:
  - Release tension
  - Discharge defensiveness
  - Express feelings.

- Keep in mind that you do not have to laugh at everything that others say. Have your own sense of humor. It is all right to create your own joke—something that is genuinely funny to you. Just make sure to look around while you laugh. If your humor is well received, great; if it is not, work on how to align your intent with the impact of the joke.
- Remember, it is difficult to be angry at someone who makes you laugh.

I WORK FOR THE BEST BOSS IN THE WORLD

Over the past three decades, since I started working at the age of 14, I have worked for the full gamut of supervisors. I have had supervisors who threatened me both verbally and physically, and I have had supervisors with whom I remain friends many years later. I have had supervisors who were micromanagers, and others who were missing in action. I've had supervisors who were competent, caring, communicative, honest, trustworthy, efficient, reliable, smart, supportive, and pleasant. Conversely, I have had supervisors who were unethical, incompetent, chaotic, mean, irritating, absent, inexperienced, unknowledgable, egotistical, backstabbing, and well, you get the picture. Supervisors come in all shapes and sizes. They are of every ethnicity. They are both men and women. They are of every age. They espouse classical management styles, modern management styles, and every management style in between. In short, supervisors are just as diverse as the populations of workers they supervise.

For me, a supervisor who trusts that I will do my job and do it well—and gives me the space and resources to do it—is by far the best supervisor. This type of supervisor realizes, often intuitively, that this is the way to get the highest quality work out of me. A supervisor whose values are in alignment with mine usually fares well too. However, just because this type of supervision works well for me doesn't mean it will work well for someone else. Supervision, like everything else, needs to be customized to the organization, the job, the team, and each individual worker. There is no one best type of supervisor. Someone I consider to be the "best" supervisor in the world could be a complete nightmare to someone else.

From my view, effective supervisors know their employees well enough to understand what motivates them and what their strengths are. They are good listeners and they have the ability to remove the "white noise" in the organization so that employees can focus on their assigned tasks. They advocate for their employees and help them grow in their jobs. They are ethical and accountable for their actions. A supervisor who possesses these attributes can supervise virtually anyone in any job domain in any organization.

More to Think About and Try

- What if your supervisor knew what motivated you? What if she knew that you did your best work when left alone with challenging tasks? What if she knew that time off to spend with your family was more important to you than a promotion that included a new title, a raise, and more responsibility that would keep you away from your family? What if she knew that as long as you were treated and compensated fairly you would do anything to ensure the customer was happy?
- What if your supervisor was an advocate for you? What if he stood up for you to others, supporting your work? What if he worked with you to identify appropriate work

tasks and developmental activities? What if he made new opportunities available to you as you grew in your job? What if he listened to you when you found a problem with a work process and worked with you to find a good solution? What if your supervisor filtered out agency politics, enabling you to focus on your assigned tasks?

- Keep these questions in mind as you shape your supervisory style to help your employees reach their potential and enjoy coming to work every day.

5

Making Good Things Happen

Getting the
Best Work
from Others

SUPERVISION

**Making
Good Things
Happen**

In Chapter 5 our focus turns to making good things happen. The stories in this chapter are about how supervisors create the environment and guide the process of getting work done to serve the mission of the organization and achieve desired outcomes. Good things happen when supervisors know how to create value for others and for their organization.

Each story in Chapter 5 has current and future relevance to supervisors across government organizations. The voices of the supervisors you hear in each story reflect real-life experiences and thoughts they want to share with you. It is our hope that you will find practical ideas to try out as you engage in your own supervisory work.

Many more stories have yet to be written about the important work of supervising others to make important things happen. One way you can give back to other supervisors is to share your stories and learning with them. At the end of this chapter is a place for you to capture some of your story ideas to share with others when an opportunity or situation presents itself.

KNOW YOUR ORGANIZATION'S PRIORITIES

Confused, overwhelmed supervisors often ask, "What's the priority?" The all-too-predictable punt—"It's all a priority!"— usually masks deeper problems related to resource allocation.

It also reflects a failure of strategy. Strategy defines and declares at a high level what the organization is going to do and, by implication, what it will not do. The strategy is real, putting big stakes in the ground around what will happen. Strategy takes a risk and commits the organization.

But this is not enough. Most supervisors would agree that there is a big difference between what is set forth as priorities and what work actually gets done. There is often a gap between the written goals and the reality of the day-to-day work. What can you do if you find yourself in this situation?

One practice I have found to be effective is "clear seeing." This practice starts with fully comprehending what is actually happening. It's important to suspend judgment in this phase. The goal is to simply notice and understand, not evaluate. Observe behaviors, actions, and decisions, and also try to broaden and deepen your frames of reference. This may mean gaining a better understanding of what is happening around you—or higher up or lower down in the hierarchy. It may mean noticing how energy and attention consistently migrate to certain areas.

In one organization where I worked, a great deal of energy and attention were spent on strategy formulation and high-level plans for marketing, sales, and technology. Yet, what people did on a day-to-day basis reflected something very different: The organization's real priority was to achieve a growth target each month. The grandest of plans would collapse under the pressure of "making the number." Once I grasped this, I was in a much better position to understand the organization's real priorities.

Once you observe what is, you are in a position to focus on what really matters. The conversation you have with your team should form the basis for creating an understanding and agreement on where the focus needs to be; then, together, you can figure out where to start.

A quality I've observed in highly effective supervisors over the years is the ability to talk openly with their teams, being candid about problem areas. Maybe processes aren't working, more resources are needed, or customer service is not strong. When asked about these deficiencies, they don't sweep them under the rug or engage in mental gymnastics to defend them. Instead, they acknowledge the problems and make clear whether they can be addressed now or later. In making this distinction, they are prioritizing, leading, and clarifying. This is a behavior that supervisors at any level can adopt.

More to Think About and Try

- Once you are sure about what really matters, the communication effort is much easier; it's about clarity, consistency, and repetition. People sometimes need to

> hear a message several times before fully committing to it, so persistence matters.
> - Take time to explain very clearly the "whys" behind the "whats." Let people know how their work affects the larger picture. And be sure to ask for their perspectives on how work could be improved in service of the big picture.

SIMPLIFYING WORK

Doing more with fewer resources is the norm in most workplaces, and while "work smarter, not harder" is overused, working smarter may be the best way to simplify work. We can do that, however, only when we are aware of subtle cues that the work our staff is doing may be going off track—even when it is on schedule.

Josh's communications office was tasked with developing a technical manual describing the processes and procedures for users of the new ERP system that was being implemented in his agency. Josh had three direct reports working on the project: Marcia, a technical writer; Stefan, the project manager; and Carlos, who provided administrative, production, and editorial support to the small team. At the outset the team met with Richard, the program manager on the ERP implementation, to identify the requirements for the manual and its purpose. Richard wanted to give users a manual that would support a smooth transition to the new system.

The team spent two weeks developing an outline of the manual based on Richard's requirements. The last time Carlos worked with an internal customer, the requirements kept changing, so he made sure that Stefan had Richard sign off on the outline. Supervisor Josh was aware that the last few projects his staff worked on were delivered late. He was worried about being seen as ineffectual by his boss, so he was determined that this project be delivered on time.

Josh met weekly with his staff to assess progress and made a point of going around the cubes daily and asking his staff how the work was going. While he thought this was showing support for his staff, they knew what he meant: "I'm worried about this project: Are you staying on schedule?" They began to focus more and more on the project milestones.

While the work seemed to be going smoothly, Marcia sensed a disconnect between what Richard said he wanted and what she was learning about the users and their needs. Richard seemed to be outlining processes that were more pertinent to his implementation team than to the day-to-day work of the system users. Marcia mentioned a few times to Stefan and Carlos that she wasn't sure the manual was on target. She even said this to Josh in passing, but he was so focused on meeting deadlines that he dismissed Marcia's concerns with "I'm sure it will be great." In his view, the project was on time and there was no need to think beyond that.

Richard had a team of users review the manual. One of them told Richard that he thought it was interesting, but of little use to him. Richard then met with Josh and asked how his team was going to "fix" the problem. Since Marcia already sensed what was going on, the team was able to recover and deliver a serviceable manual for the users. But this effort required considerable rework, and the project was completed late.

As supervisors, if we keep the focus exclusively on productivity—on getting things done—we limit our ability, and our staff's ability, to recognize and solve problems. Nothing complicates work more than spending time and effort in the wrong places. Timelines, milestones, deadlines, and project plans are necessary tools for getting work done, yet focus on these tools to the exclusion of what else is going on with our staff, the customer, and the work can lead us down the path of doing the "wrong" work—the work that in the end doesn't achieve what we need it to achieve.

More to Think About and Try

- *Recognize project plans and work outlines for what they are*—plans and outlines. It is important to reexamine them periodically and revise them if they are no longer relevant.
- *Pay attention to your staff's side comments about their work.* Even if you would rather not hear them, they may signal what's actually going on more than formal weekly meetings do.
- *Ask yourself if you are focusing too much on controlling your staff's work.* If you are, plan agenda-less get-togethers with staff. While they may violate the "rules" of holding effective meetings, more informal discussions will often surface both problems and solutions.

BEING CLEAR ABOUT EXPECTATIONS

I was fairly new in my position and was tasked with putting together and submitting a very important planning document for our organization. The compilation of a great deal of data, the TBA (Table of Distribution and Allowance) affects the requirements—human resources as well as material needs—for our group. This planning document would enable us to meet the annual submittal for resource requirements. Although I understood the importance of the document and was generally familiar with its function, I had never been responsible for developing and submitting the TBA.

I received the assignment with few instructions. I wasn't provided with any references or supporting regulations. I was led to believe that the window for completing this assignment was very small. Although I was initially concerned, I quickly appreciated the latitude I had been given and decided to embrace the initiative.

I knew I had to gather information from many areas of our organization; since I believed the time to complete this task was limited, I didn't want to waste any of it. I felt that I didn't have the time to root out detailed instructions and guidelines. I moved ahead quickly.

After expending an inordinate amount of time and energy, I learned that the timeline was much longer than I had been told. Not only that, but portions of the report didn't have to done every year. Most important, instructions were available that countered many of my assumptions—and much of what I had put in the original draft document.

Though painful, this learning experience has helped me be a better supervisor. It has made me more cognizant of the need to be thorough about giving instructions or guidance to my team. I pay more attention to describing what needs to be done and when it needs to be done. I think more about all the stakeholders who might be involved and how they can contribute to the success of the project. I also try to instill in my direct reports that it is their responsibility to know what is expected of them, ask for details initially, check their assumptions periodically, and seek clarification as a task or project unfolds to avoid wasting time and energy.

More to Think About and Try

- Think "stretch" when setting expectations.
- Tie expectations to the strategic goals of the organization.

- Get commitment and connect expectations to accountability.
- Have regular, to-the-point conversations with your direct reports throughout the year.
- Ask questions to ensure understanding and listen for concerns and frustrations.
- Acknowledge success.

MY SUPERVISOR IS NEVER AROUND

I had taken a job that I liked, working closely with a great supervisor. After about a year, my supervisor took on additional responsibilities that caused him to split his time between two unrelated roles. As is often the case with new responsibilities, much of my supervisor's time was increasingly devoted to learning the ropes of his new role. While I was happy for my supervisor and understood that the new role was important to our organization, a problem soon emerged for me: My supervisor was never around.

Initially, I was unsure how to proceed with my own job responsibilities without regular input from my supervisor. We had worked closely together and I had become accustomed to seeking out his opinion on a routine basis. Also, we worked in a deadline-driven environment and part of his customary role was to give the go-ahead before I proceeded with scheduled work.

In view of the increased demands of my supervisor's new responsibilities, I knew that my role would have to change. I began to exercise greater leadership over our shared work. Fortunately

I had spent enough time in my role that I knew the job well and understood the responsibilities. Rather than waiting for my supervisor to provide input on minor issues, I started making day-to-day decisions independently. This helped us stay on schedule despite my supervisor's absences. Soon, I began to see my supervisor's absences as an opportunity rather than a problem—an opportunity to take ownership of my job responsibilities.

I still needed some outside input, however. I began building closer relationships with other coworkers with the goal of establishing a support network. Although we did not work specifically on the same projects, they understood the work and, if my supervisor was not available at a critical time, they could provide guidance and assistance where needed.

Of course, I needed to keep my supervisor apprised of my work. I began sending him regular email updates to keep him informed about my day-to-day work, the status of our projects, and any upcoming deadlines. I also scheduled weekly in-person meetings to give him a high-level overview of my work and to seek his input when I needed assistance. This structure helped us stay in contact without overburdening either of our schedules; in addition, it allowed us to plan for and ultimately meet our deadlines.

Importantly, my supervisor gave me plenty of positive feedback on my newfound decisiveness and my consequent ability to keep our projects moving forward when he wasn't available. I knew he appreciated my efforts to take greater ownership of our shared work. Ultimately, the situation worked out well for both of us: He was promoted into a full-time role related to the new responsibilities he had taken on and, because I had demonstrated that I was able to exercise greater leadership in my position, I was promoted into his former supervisory role.

More to Think About and Try

- *What if I had not taken the initiative* to step up and assume greater independence and responsibility? Chances are, my supervisor and I would both have been frustrated, stressed, and unhappy—and likely not promoted into our new roles.
- *What if I had been afraid to make decisions* and had persisted in waiting for direction from my supervisor? I might have been viewed as lazy, disinterested, or simply incapable of fulfilling my job responsibilities. I certainly would not have been promoted into my new role.
- *You'll rarely regret stepping up to the task at hand* or taking the leap into a new role—but you will almost always regret not doing so.

OUR WORK AND LEARNING STYLES ARE DIFFERENT

I have been at my current grade and in my current position for several years. My responsibilities include a wide range of tasks that require me to be in contact with a variety of divisions within the agency. The tasks for which I am responsible are very visible. If I do my job well, other people see it and if I screw up, they see that too. I have good rapport with my supervisor and I am given a lot of independence because he would know immediately if I weren't doing my job effectively. I have received very good performance reviews, and I have taken that as a signal that he approves of how I work as well as what I have accomplished.

Although I enjoy my job, I had been getting bored with the day-to-day tasks. When my supervisor called me in to talk about a temporary assignment, I couldn't have been happier. This assignment would be on a project that was scheduled to last more than a year. It would be carried out at my location so I didn't have to worry about changing work locations or commuting farther to work.

My supervisor explained that I was selected specifically because I am able to work independently within the general guidelines of a project. This project involved coordinating a lot of different resources within various segments of the organization.

As I found out more about the assignment I became more and more excited. The team on this project would be led by a "legend" in the field. She had credentials a mile long in her technical field and was always quoted at meetings and conferences. This legend was going to be my direct supervisor. I looked at this as a real opportunity to contribute something new to my organization and also to learn from this leader in the field.

The first few weeks were rough, but I wasn't too worried about the growing tension I felt because we were just getting work arrangements figured out. As we went into the third and fourth months, though, I knew something was very wrong. I'm used to the typical reporting requirements of a government organization, but my new supervisor was imposing numerous extra reports and updates on the group. I thought they were unnecessary and were taking valuable time away from the task at hand.

More specifically, I was having trouble with her looking over my shoulder and second-guessing my decisions. She was making me feel like she did not trust me to do my job, and I was unable to tell whether she realized she was giving me that impression.

I asked for a meeting and put together some notes so I would stay on topic and be clear about my concerns. During the meeting

I pointed out specific instances where I believed my work was hindered by her scrutiny and noted that she was not getting the best out of me by reviewing every decision I made. I also showed how the reports she was requesting duplicated material already being communicated.

She listened politely and seemed to genuinely listen to me. Then she said, "Well, that's the way I work. My reputation is on the line and I am going to continue to be very careful about what is done by each member of this group. So, you'll have to find a way to work in this environment."

I spent some time reflecting on my situation and trying to figure out if there was any way I could work well within the system she had created. My decision was that I could not. I believe that I work best when I can work independently and my supervisor believed—for her own good reasons—that she could not let me work that way.

I requested and was granted permission to leave the special project and go back to my old job. It was not a matter of right or wrong. Conflicting work and learning styles can mean the difference between success or failure on a project or task.

More to Think About and Try

- *What if I had done more investigation about the person leading the project as a supervisor?* I probably would have learned about her working and supervisory style. I didn't look beyond her technical skills. I also should have better assessed my own needs and styles.
- *What if I wanted to give it a try and stay with the project team until the project was complete?* I would have

needed to find new ways keep my spirit up while getting my work done. One thing I could have done was ask my supervisor to sit down with me to review my work so she could give me feedback on the spot; at the same time I would have learned a little more about her thought process.

UNDERSTANDING YOUR WORK ENVIRONMENT

I have been in my current position in the middle of my organization for several years and have worked for the government most of my career. By this time I should realize that in the government there will be decisions about which I have no say.

My supervisor has an open door policy and I feel comfortable sharing my opinions and ideas with him. My group has been instrumental in pushing forward a lot of important initiatives, and I have always felt that we are valued across the organization.

I had begun to believe that I actually controlled more aspects of my situation than I did.

Like most government organizations, my group has limited resources. Adding to staff is not easy and usually takes time and a lot of work. I had been lobbying for a new position to be added to our team and supplied my supervisor with the facts and the paperwork to support this. We met and discussed the staff addition and he expressed complete support.

Some weeks later I was informed that a new staff member would be added—but not for the position I had lobbied for. When I spoke with my supervisor, he said that this was not something within our control. He remarked that the decision was made higher up.

I was frustrated. I then realized that this is part of working for the government. There are always going to be policies, issues, and actions over which I will have no control or input. I have to realize that my supervisor is also in a position where he may not be able influence those above him. However, that doesn't mean we're going to stop trying.

More to Think About and Try

- Understand what you can and cannot control in your work environment.
- Pay attention to timing when you put an idea forward; expect to get a reaction.
- Identify the stakeholders and learn about their perspectives: Who are the supporters? Who are the resisters?
- Try to find some common ground or shared interests.
- Use your leadership skills to establish your credibility and energize supporters to help you take steps to realize your idea.

BUILDING STRONG RELATIONSHIPS

"Success in most jobs depends on our ability to cultivate, manage, and grow relationships with executives, peers, and subordinates." I was a new supervisor and these were the first words I heard from my well-known supervisor. I felt honored to work with her and knew I would learn a great deal.

"Just remember," she said, "managing professional relationships requires expert navigational skills, a deft understanding of motivational tactics, and an ability to build coalitions, often where none exist." Impressive language, I thought. I had questions, but I responded affirmatively.

My supervisor, who was in charge of a multi-organizational council composed of top federal executives, called on me to act as team lead for a group of fellow supervisors to help execute her priorities. She said it was critical to hit the ground running so she helped me develop a series of short-, medium-, and long-range goals:

- Short-range: Understand the strategic direction of the organization and successfully implement goals to manage daily operations.
- Medium-range: Make the organization visible.
- Long-range: Solidify a positive legacy.

She further advised me, "Regardless of your place in an organization, it is always a good idea to identify your colleagues, customers, and stakeholders and meet with them to develop a connection, learn their interests, and communicate your vision and expectations for your job." "And," she noted, "here's the risk. If you rest on your laurels, trust can become tenuous and goodwill can evaporate." With this warning, I took the next steps to help her solidify credibility by generating early wins.

"To be successful," she advised, "involve colleagues in action planning." Like many feds, we had limited resources and a tight budget. She warned me, "Pick your targets. Start with the easy ones to learn how to make success happen. Work with colleagues in agencies where we have strong connections and then move across government to collaborate. We need to work together to achieve the long-range goals."

This sage advice I received early in my career has served me well as I have moved to new and more challenging supervisory positions. No matter at what level you are serving as a supervisor, relationships matter.

More to Think About and Try

- Seek input from others.
- Listen openly to others' ideas.
- Share information and perspectives freely.
- Ask questions to learn and appreciate others' views.
- Communicate often and with intent.

SEEKING GUIDANCE

I have long believed that the worst thing that can happen is nothing. I often consider this when weighing the potential outcomes of any decision, from trying a new recipe to seeking guidance from a superior at work. I would prefer to try something and fail, taking the learning experience in stride, than to remain stagnant. Nothing would ever happen if we did not take risks, try new things, or challenge ourselves. This was, unfortunately, exactly the situation when I felt powerless in my workplace. Nothing happened when I consciously chose not to seek guidance from my supervisor, or her supervisors, when I felt there was a need for improvement in our working environment.

As a graduate student, I worked as an assistant to an international fellowship exchange program. This was the perfect opportunity for me to develop professional skills and to apply what I was learning in the classroom to a real-world setting. I was originally hired by a program coordinator who had a wealth of cross-cultural experience; I was to collaborate with her as an equal throughout the year to organize professional development opportunities, manage intercultural exchange activities, and provide support to our international guests. Shortly after I started, she left her position and was replaced by someone I was expected to work *for* instead of *with*. This posed an immediate challenge in our two-person office. Within a few weeks of the new coordinator's arrival, the program's established ideals of collaboration and exchange quickly crumbled—just as our year-long guests arrived on U.S. soil, excited about their year abroad.

When the international fellows arrived, they were greeted with a two-week orientation that set their expectations high, promising professional development opportunities, guaranteed class schedules, and numerous cultural-exchange activities. Given these high expectations, the group determined that we would need to maintain open lines of communication. We verbally established a culture of trust and safety among the group that welcomed all feedback and suggestions. What was discussed, however, was never put into practice.

Before long, participants began confiding in me that they did not feel that the program coordinator was approachable for guidance or advice, particularly as they adjusted to a new country, school, language, and culture. I became concerned about our group's dynamic and about our role in managing and upholding their expectations. What should I do? Should I have a conversation with the coordinator, knowing that my previous attempts to seek guidance had been met with defensiveness and anger—and that she had chastised me for not taking initiative? Should I take the initiative to organize additional meetings and activities for the participants, knowing that my previous attempts to take initiative had resulted in the coordinator accusing me of going behind her back? Should I talk with the coordinator anyway and plan to seek guidance from her superiors if she failed to take my concerns seriously? This was quite a conundrum. Of course, there was another option, which was the one I chose: Do nothing. I did nothing because I feared for my job.

This organizational culture clearly did not encourage seeking guidance as a means of growth and learning. It was a hierarchical structure that lacked the transparency and safety we hoped to project for our international participants. It was an environment in which I never dared to share ideas, make suggestions, or seek guidance. I did what I was told because I knew if I did otherwise, I would be reprimanded or perhaps terminated. I often reflect upon this experience when thinking about what I do not want from a working environment: conditions that foster apathy and disengagement.

I wish I had known then what I know now about coaching and influencing up rather than silently counting the days until my contract ended. I also wish I had taken the risk to seek guidance from my supervisor—or her supervisors. Even if my efforts had been unsuccessful, at least I would have felt that I had tried. Instead, I did nothing to improve my time with the fellowship, and worse, I did nothing to improve the fellows' year in the United States.

More to Think About and Try

- *Communicate your expectations clearly;* listen carefully to your direct reports' questions so you can clarify as needed.
- *Encourage your direct reports to share their observations* and experiences so improvements can be made when needed.
- *Check in periodically with your direct reports* to make sure they have what they need to accomplish their work.
- *Seek feedback from your direct reports* on how you can better support them in completing their work.
- *Periodically join your direct reports* where the work is being done to create openings for asking questions, getting clarification, and addressing challenges.

MISTAKES WILL HAPPEN

I must admit that I have made my share of mistakes over my years as a supervisor. Mistakes are inevitable even with seasoned and experienced supervisors because supervision involves making decisions based on anticipation of how others will behave—and that is more of an art than a science. Furthermore, supervisory decisions are sometimes made under pressure to resolve an immediate problem without the luxury of time to carefully consider the implications. The important thing is that we glean valuable lessons from mistakes and errors that we can apply in future situations.

I have spent my career in the field of finance and accounting and I have often experienced high staff turnover as a result of poor performance, excessive workload, insecurity caused by budgetary constraints, and other factors. Although these situations are certainly not unique to finance and accounting, supervising employees with fiduciary responsibilities has a unique facet. When essential functions absolutely must be done in a nonflexible timeframe, the temptation is to hire quickly to "get a body in the seat" and get the job done. Such was the case with one of my first hires as a new supervisor. Abby was the accounts payable clerk I hired to fill an unexpected vacancy. She seemed to have the necessary technical skills and I needed to get the organization's invoices paid, so I hired her and got her on board as quickly as possible.

"Sandy, I think we are missing some blank checks out of our check stock," Rex informed me one Friday evening just before closing time. My staff was small and Rex, a long-time employee, occasionally acted as backup for other employees. "Really?" I asked in disbelief. I knew I was responsible for dealing with this situation promptly, so I proceeded to investigate the matter over the weekend. I quickly discerned that Abby had indeed forged and cashed checks in the last couple of days. On Monday, I confronted her with the evidence and, of course, she initially denied it. After further questioning she tearfully conceded that she had perpetrated the fraud. Fortunately, because the theft was caught quickly, we sustained only a small financial loss. However, the consequent legal proceedings involved a substantial amount of valuable staff time.

From this single experience I learned multiple valuable lessons.

The first lesson is to take the necessary time to find the best candidate for the job, even if it means doing the job yourself in the interim or engaging a qualified expert on a temporary basis. Finding a candidate with the right values, skills, and disposition is worth the short-term pain of having the position vacant.

The second lesson I learned is to hold employees accountable for their actions. When I first confronted Abby with the evidence of her fraud, she broke down in tears and truly seemed regretful for what she had done. She was in a terrible home situation and needed the money. I am a very compassionate person and was momentarily tempted to not hold her accountable for her actions. Fortunately, the human relations director working with me helped me avoid that mistake.

The third lesson is to "trust, but verify." This was Ronald Reagan's signature phrase with regard to Soviet relations. At face value, this approach seems self-contradictory, but it simply implies that trust should not be blind trust. Even though good internal controls and procedures are in place to prevent fraud, it is important to keep your eyes open to the possibility that these controls can be circumvented and that good people can do bad things when under pressure.

The last lesson relates directly to the importance of having a dedicated team of employees. Fortunately, Rex was a team player and was motivated to disclose the information that led to detection of the fraud immediately.

More to Think About and Try

- *Acknowledge mistakes.* Acknowledge personally, and to superiors as appropriate, that a mistake has been made. Be straight up about it.
- *Take responsibility for actions.* Assume personal responsibility for the mistake and take the necessary action to correct the mistake to the degree possible.
- *Learn.* Consider the mistake a valuable lesson and avoid repeating it in the future.
- *Share with others.* Share the experience with others in similar positions to help them avoid making the same mistake.

THE COST OF NEGATIVITY

Negativity in the workplace is something we have all experienced at some point in our careers. When negative attitudes and behaviors become the norm rather than the exception, the impact on productivity and morale can be devastating. Negativity can come from one member of one division or it can emanate from a larger faction of dissatisfied employees in multiple divisions. Negativity is contagious; common manifestations are gossip, hostility, pessimism, complaining, and resistance to change.

There may be nothing more toxic to a team than persistent negativity because it takes focus away from critical tasks and drains the team's energy. When employees are distracted by a need to devote time and energy to dealing with negative team members, there is an opportunity cost for the organization.

No matter the cause, negativity must be dealt with quickly. Here is a story that illustrates how one supervisor dealt with negativity on his team.

Larry supervised a team of six designers responsible for creating intellectual properties for the organization's customers. Sarah was the newest member of the team and was eager to learn from her supervisor and others. She was creative and outgoing, making her a good fit on the team. She was given clear direction about her responsibilities and the type of work expected of her. She started off working closely with Larry and asking questions along the way. Larry was eager to see her first deliverables.

After a month, Larry noticed that Sarah's questions hadn't abated. In fact, the same questions came up again and again and the tone of those questions was increasingly negative. Sarah continually expressed frustration with her team members and the organization's procedures for design projects. Each time, Larry reinforced the roles and responsibilities of the team members, the need to work well with others, and the organization's requirement to follow certain protocols and processes. He clearly stated his expectation that Sarah work on her communication style with the team and continue to follow organizational processes.

Sarah's questions soon began to include negative statements about why none of the design projects would be successful. Larry was often pulled from his own work to advise others on her project team who were having difficulty working with her. Sarah began gossiping with others, spreading her negative attitudes about others in the organization. The quality and timeliness of the entire team's work declined, and Sarah spent more time complaining to others than she spent working on projects. The negativity became so pervasive that Sarah and another team member stopped speaking to one another.

Determined to get to the root cause, Larry sat down with Sarah to hear her concerns. She was unhappy because she felt ignored and undervalued by the team. He then met with the entire design team to allow all members an opportunity to vent their frustrations. He was able to help the team identify several things they could do to improve their communication on projects, give all members an opportunity for input, and allow them to work better as a team. Larry also looked for opportunities to create fun for the team, whether it was getting them together for a group lunch or challenging them to come up with creative ideas on projects.

Sometimes even a misunderstanding can create anxiety about the future or make an employee feel undervalued. If the root cause is not addressed, it can fester and eat away at productivity and morale.

More to Think About and Try

- *Identify negative behavior.* You must first know where the negativity is coming from. You may also want to stop and check on your own attitudes and behaviors—are you contributing to the negativity? Remember to focus on behaviors, not people.
- *Note the specific business impact.* Be specific: What are some concrete examples of lost productivity? How much time has been spent dealing with the negativity? The impacts are the symptoms of a deeper issue. Addressing one and not the other is ineffective.

- **Listen and identify alternatives.** Negativity isn't always bad; sometimes there are good reasons for it. It can bring issues to the surface and become a catalyst for a desperately needed change. The key to finding a remedy is to listen to the cause of the negativity. When all else fails, manage negativity as you would any other performance issue.

STORIES YOU WANT TO SHARE WITH OTHERS

As a supervisor you will collect many stories over the years. Some will be short stories; some will be long stories. To help you capture the stories you will want to share with others when the time is right, we have created some space for you to jot down story facts and reflections. Over time we all misplace knowledge. Here is a simple tool to help you understand, process, and remember some important stories about supervising others.

Story #1

Unique Story Title: _____

Highlights of the Situation:

_____

_____

_____

_____

Reflections and Learning Points to Share:

_____

_____

_____

_____

Story #2

Unique Story Title: _____

Highlights of the Situation:

_____

_____

_____

_____

Reflections and Learning Points to Share:

_____

_____

_____

_____

Story #3

Unique Story Title: _____

Highlights of the Situation:

_____

_____

_____

_____

Reflections and Learning Points to Share:

_____

_____

_____

_____

Supervising in a Changing Work Landscape

If someone asked you to write a quick story describing the work you do and how you do it compared to five years ago, or even two years ago, what changes would you highlight in your story? Would you mention non-stop emails, team projects, new tools to connect you 24/7, web meetings? The truth is, your work and your workplace are changing in ways that impact how you go about doing your work each and every day.

By nature, you are likely more comfortable with in an easy-flowing work environment—being able to make choices about what to pay attention to and what actions to take without thinking much about it. However, as a supervisor, you have an opportunity to embrace the forces of change that are happening in your work environment. Three specific actions will make your approach to supervising in a changing work landscape more valuable and fulfilling:

- Be aware of your current work culture.
- Know your gaps in capability.
- Continue to learn and develop.

Following discussion of these actions, you will find six stories that illustrate aspects of the changing work landscape. Our intent is to help you gain new or different ways of thinking about the ripple effect of a changing work landscape. You will also find some practical ways to embrace the forces of change that will affect you as a supervisor.

BEING AWARE OF YOUR CURRENT WORK CULTURE

Work culture is the environment that surrounds you at work and is represented by the values, attitudes, behaviors, and assumptions of the individuals that make up the organization. The work culture shapes your work practices, relationships, work processes, and workspace.

In your organization, what is the "centerpiece" of your current work culture? How do individuals interact with each other? What are the relationships among technology, people, and processes in terms of getting work done? What are the relationships among and between people? What topics do you *not* hear in conversations that might be indicators of the work culture?

Answering these questions will help you determine the best way to supervise both the work itself and the people doing the work in a changing environment. You will begin to see how your understanding of the work culture helps you respond in new ways to getting work done through others. You will realize how one part of the work culture affects another. You will become aware of how collaborative and virtual technology is causing work and life activities to intermingle. You will begin to see how people socialize as they work on a shared or parallel activity to reach a common goal. By recognizing the many forces of change in your work culture, you will find it easier to understand how one part of the culture affects another.

KNOWING YOUR GAPS IN CAPABILITY

Once you know your current capabilities in the context of your work and the changing work environment, it will be easier to determine if you need to update or acquire any new capabilities. A good way to assess your current capabilities is to look at them from three different perspectives: (1) the strength of your foundational skills, (2) your comfort with using technology tools, and (3) your contextual awareness of your surroundings.

Some things never change. Foundational skills are the core skills you need to supervise well in any situation. Can you communicate clearly and persuasively? Can you interpret information? Can you present ideas succinctly? Can you think critically and creatively? Are you able to solve problems?

Technology tools are no longer optional; they are essential to achieving most supervisory tasks in the workplace today. Do you use technology tools to increase your productivity? Do you use collaboration tools to learn and interact with peers, experts, and others? Can you easily locate, collect, and evaluate information from various sources using technology? Do you use technology resources to solve problems and make decisions?

Contextual awareness opens up a new way of seeing the world that surrounds you as a supervisor. How open are you to exploring new things? How easy is it for you to identify patterns and connections? Do you look for underlying issues when confronting situations? Do you pay attention to the interrelationships of things? How easy is it for you to put aside accepted beliefs or constraints?

Your answers to these questions can serve as a starting point for identifying the gaps you may want to close as you strive to become more effective supervising in a changing work environment. By understanding and preparing yourself to work in the new and emerging environments, you will be better prepared to support others as they embrace changes in their work and the work setting.

CONTINUING TO LEARN AND DEVELOP

When you view learning and development as a continuous process, it is easier to find ways to engage in experiences that will help you focus on making changes over time. To gain more exposure to changing supervisory situations, you may want to consider both formal and informal learning opportunities. Varied experiences through projects, new initiatives, and problem scenarios provide great opportunities to learn and experiment with different behaviors. To make these types of learning experiences possible in your government environment, you may need to challenge yourself to consider new ways of organizing and sharing resources.

You can also learn from seasoned truths shared by supervisors or others who have come to know your organization through ups and downs. This source of insight can help you navigate through ambiguities that get in the way of seeing new possibilities for change. Learning lessons from the experiences of others is one of the most powerful ways to create new discussions and help others see things in new ways.

WORKERS IN DIFFERENT LOCATIONS

Today's workers are often not in the same location as their supervisor or their colleagues. In many agencies, workers are located in different buildings in the same city, around the country, and even worldwide. Yet the collaborative nature of work requires that these dispersed workers accomplish a mutual goal. In addition, the federal government is increasingly relying on telework as a means for workers to accomplish work from locations other than their office.

Nicholas was a senior, GS-14, supervisor who was overseeing three IT projects for his agency, each for a different department or bureau that was in a different building in Washington, D.C. His staff were experienced technical employees who reported to work at their respective project locations. Initially Nicholas visited each team once or twice a week; that dropped off after a few weeks as he began to get busy with other work at his office, which was located in the agency's headquarters building.

After a few months, the projects began to run into technical issues. The team members began asking Nicholas questions about whether their counterparts were experiencing the same problems, and, if so, what they were doing to fix them. As the supervisor and senior technical expert, Nicholas felt that it was up to him to solve the problems. In his words, "I designed this technical approach and the team is not doing a very good job putting it into action. I should be able to find a solution and then tell them the answer."

Maureen, a senior IT specialist for one of the teams, had a different viewpoint. Nicholas had not adjusted the project schedule, even though it was delayed as a result of the technical issues, and he wasn't asking for the team's input. Moreover, she was the one who had to keep the customer—the deputy undersecretary of the department—happy on a daily basis.

One evening, Maureen called Henry, a close colleague on one of the other projects. They talked for two hours, sharing the technical problems and expressing frustration with Nicholas' inaction. They wondered whether the third team was having the same problems, but neither of them knew any of those employees well enough to give them a call.

The following week, Henry and Maureen met after work several times to map out some possible solutions. They came up with a few viable solutions and agreed that they would test them out at their project sites. The next day, Maureen spent most of the morning trying one of the new solutions while working through lunch to finish her regular project work. She was confident that the solution would work!

That afternoon, Nicholas unexpectedly stopped by. Maureen was excited about solving a major technical problem, so she shared the news with Nicholas. She said, "Henry and I have taken the initiative to find a solution. I know this will work and will get our projects back on schedule."

Nicholas' immediate reaction was that Maureen and Henry had overstepped their bounds. It was up to him—not them—to lead these projects. Nicholas told Maureen, "Your solution won't work, and you shouldn't have gone behind my back by calling team meetings. I want you to stop all work on this project until we can get it under control. And, I'm going to have to have a talk with Henry." Maureen was devastated.

Her teammates knew what had happened—they were working in tight spaces and it was impossible to keep anything secret. Maureen's colleagues shared similar frustrations. They weren't sure who was in charge of the project when Nicholas wasn't around, they felt out of touch with their colleagues at headquarters, and they had to work long hours to keep up on their other job duties. Maureen saw some signs that their morale had dropped—coming in late, working from home whenever possible, and spending time griping about the project—which confirmed that they were just as frustrated as she was.

More to Think About and Try

- *How do you think Maureen feels about Nicholas's style of supervision?* What could Nicholas have done differently to lead these three teams? Think specifically about how Nicholas could have set expectations differently and communicated differently. How does this approach differ from supervising employees who are in a single location?

- *Managing workers in different locations presents some unique but addressable challenges.* You may not be around when your employees need you to make a decision or would like to share information with you. When employees are not able to interact with each other easily or in a timely manner, it becomes difficult for them to share lessons learned or build cohesion. One thing you can do is set expectations about when and where you will interact with your employees, and then stick to it. Get input from your employees on their expectations. Is a weekly status meeting frequent enough?

Too frequent? Can they call or email you when needed? In the evenings?

- **Set expectations about the role and authority of each person on your team.** Think about designating a "site lead" who can make certain decisions in your absence. Decide how you will facilitate interactions among employees at different sites—for example, will you use an email list/group to share technical problems and answers?

THE CHANGING WORLD OF SOCIAL CONNECTIONS

These days, most people have at least a passing knowledge of what social media is, even if they don't personally have a Facebook, LinkedIn, or Twitter account. The use of social media in a professional or work setting is newer, though, and is still evolving as a vital tool for organizations. Supervisors who may be perfectly comfortable communicating with friends via their Facebook page may not feel comfortable posting comments or otherwise engaging in conversations on their organization's site, let alone participating in a blog discussion. I learned the hard way that supervisors who (1) do not feel confident about how to use social media, (2) are unsure how to use it in a professional context, or (3) don't trust their staff with public, online communication may inhibit their direct reports from participating in new ways of communicating.

Tasked with launching the social media program for my organization, I was responsible not only for developing our externally facing social networks but also for encouraging staff participation. We wanted our staff to get involved and we wanted them to participate in our new online communities to showcase our customer focus and level of expertise.

I planned a series of informational brown bag sessions with a social media expert to acclimate our staff to the uses and potentials of social media for our organization. We provided a set of legally sanctioned rules for professional participation in online communities based on best practices that were readily available on the web from a variety of sources. The rules provided commonsense guidelines and legal protection for the company.

Participation in the sessions was lower than expected; only about 10 percent of the staff attended. This came as a surprise, given the high interest expressed across the company in launching the latest communication platform.

Additionally, while I had expected employees to be enthusiastic about using the new media, I instead found widespread concern about participating individually. Even with the rules in hand, people were unsure what to do next. Many of those who attended the informational meeting had no problem using the media in their private lives but were reluctant to do so in the context of the organization.

Much of the apprehension centered around the separation of their private life from their professional life. The use of social media in a professional setting blurred the line for them. Some voiced concern that they didn't want to "get in trouble" if information from their personal Facebook page somehow showed up on the organization's Facebook page.

Another challenge was time: Many staff members felt they didn't have enough hours in the day to monitor and respond to information exchanges within our social networks.

In the course of investigating why our launch elicited such low participation, I found that several supervisors had conveyed to their staff that using social media was somehow "unprofessional." One supervisor went so far as to direct his staff not to participate. I had mistakenly assumed that supervisors would review our social media strategy and guidelines, and then encourage their staff to participate within the context of their jobs.

Everything about social media is evolving quickly; if I had launched this same program a few months later, I might not have encountered these problems. Job-relevant networking sites that separate private and professional settings are helping break down these barriers.

Perhaps the most valuable lesson I learned is that supervisors must be on board from day one. Supervisors can and do influence the behaviors and attitudes of their team, directly impacting any project that calls for team participation.

More to Think About and Try

- Be transparent and do not hide that you work for your organization.
- Never represent yourself or the organization in a false or misleading way. All statements must be true; all claims must be substantiated.
- Post meaningful, respectful comments.
- Never participate in any social media where a controversial topic is being discussed.
- Use common sense and common courtesy.
- Stick to your area of expertise.
- When disagreeing with others' opinions, be appropriate and polite.

- If you write about other organizations, do so diplomatically. Be honest and balanced.
- Never comment on anything related to legal matters or litigation.
- Be smart about protecting yourself, your privacy, and the organization's confidential information. What you publish is widely accessible and will be around for a long time. Google has a long memory.

MAKING INFORMATION AND KNOWLEDGE SHARING EASIER

Being a supervisor is not simply about managing projects; it's about engaging with people to get meaningful things done well. To make this happen, you must get people to work together—to collaborate, both internally and externally. And to get people to work together effectively, you've got to get them to share information freely.

Several years ago when I worked in the Department of Defense, I was asked to develop a "continuity program." This effort would help keep innovative projects moving forward by capturing existing knowledge and relevant, ongoing information. Expected to take two months to develop, the program had taken almost twice as long before it was abandoned altogether. The main culprit was the unwillingness of long-tenured personnel to share their knowledge. For a variety of reasons, they did not trust the motives of the leaders who had commissioned the effort. Focusing mostly on the possibilities presented by emerging technical capability, the leadership had sorely underestimated the need to work the human side of the equation.

Knowledge sharing has been a hot topic in the workplace for the past 10 years. Most advice centers on the technical aspects of sharing information—the tools of the trade. But successful knowledge sharing happens only when the supervisor creates an environment of trust, where there's a willingness to share information. The supervisor's challenge is to help employees get past the three main motivations for withholding information: risk, power, and time.

If there's one thing that can stop effective internal communication dead in its tracks, it's the perceived risk of "putting it out there." Every time we offer information, we become accountable for what we know and for what we say we've accomplished. Others may challenge, question, and probe for understanding—and potentially expose us as less than knowledgeable.

There's also the risk that others may take credit for our information. In a work environment where there's little trust, we attach ourselves to our knowledge. We don't want to take the chance of others stealing our glory, so we keep our information to ourselves.

There's a familiar expression that "knowledge is power." We may be afraid that sharing our information with others strips us of the only power we feel we have. The truth is, only collective knowledge is power. Individual knowledge that is not shared leads to irrelevance and delayed solutions. When that knowledge is shared in a collaborative spirit, the collective understanding of issues, obstacles, and possibilities grows exponentially.

The final motivation for withholding information is that we don't have enough time to pass along what we know, given our competing priorities. This is simply shortsighted thinking.

All three motivations for withholding information—risk, power, and time—played a part in the failure of the continuity program I was helping develop. But the biggest failure was the leadership's inability to recognize the importance of the human element in making knowledge sharing successful. Had they acted differently, our continuity program would have become a reality instead of another model of failure.

More to Think About and Try

- **Be the example.** In reality, very little information is too sensitive to pass along. If you provide as much information as often as you can, your employees will trust that you're being up front and honest and they'll be more willing to share what they know with you and with others. Help your employees feel safe about sharing their knowledge.
- **Challenge ideas, not people.** If someone feels threatened by a challenge, deal with it right away. Collaborative teams challenge each other in a spirit of learning to promote the state of the art.
- **Be truthful...**about what you know and what you don't know. Truthfulness leads to trust and helps manage others' expectations of you, minimizing risk.
- **Take the long view.** Collaborative organizations recognize that everything we know is sparked by ideas born of others' hard work. Be happy to pass along your knowledge in the hopes that others will use it to accomplish breakthroughs. Reward collaborative behavior.
- **Invest your time for the future.** Sharing knowledge takes time, but it also empowers others. When knowledge is shared, more resources are available to apply to the task.
- **Realize that you're not in charge of knowledge.** The traditional hierarchical systems of management don't work with knowledge sharing. Knowledge is ever flowing and changing, so be part of the process rather than trying to control it.

◼MULTI-GENERATIONS AT WORK

Even when we share the same background and values as our coworkers, interacting with people at work can be complicated. When we work with people who are part of a different generation, our professional relationships are often even more challenging. Here's a story told by Christine, a Generation X supervisor who felt she was stuck in the middle between her Baby Boomer supervisor and her Generation Y team.

I thought highly of my team and had risen through the ranks myself so I understood the challenges of the job. The team members got their jobs because they were ambitious, hard-working, and considered to be "up and coming." All the team members were under 30 and everyone had completed or was currently in a graduate program. Our responsibilities were high-profile and therefore high-risk, but we dealt well with the fast-paced, unpredictable nature of our work.

I could tell that the team members liked each other and generally liked working for me, but I could also tell that some of them were growing dissatisfied with their positions. Melissa had been working on a project for Kathleen directly and she asked me for a quick touch-base meeting to discuss how it was going. "Christine, I was wondering if there is an opportunity to take me off the documentation project with Kathleen. I don't think I'm meeting her expectations," Melissa began.

I did not anticipate her opening. Melissa was my best coordinator and this project allowed her to network with upper management. Melissa was savvy enough to recognize the opportunity this presented. "Really? Why do you feel that way?" I asked.

"Well, I just don't think that Kathleen wants me to provide the reports. She has never given me any feedback on how I'm doing.

She insists that I print and send the reports via interoffice mail instead of just emailing them, which makes the process about a day and a half longer. The data for the reports isn't available until the 15th of the month and she wants the reports on the 17th. Three days to compile the reports even without the delivery time is already almost impossible to meet. She also gets really upset if she calls my office line and I don't happen to be sitting at my desk. I have to work overtime to get the reports done for her and I'm never late on my deadline. I don't understand why she cares when or where I do the reports as long as she gets them on time; her checking up on me is insulting."

I scheduled a meeting with Kathleen to see how she was feeling about the reports she received from Melissa. She told me she was generally pleased. After I explained some of Melissa's frustrations, Kathleen said to me, "You know, I think I have one or two more years of managing this team in me. I just don't understand the young people these days."

I was totally surprised by the comment and had no idea how to respond. It occurred to me that much of the tension between my team and Kathleen could be explained by generational issues. I explained to Kathleen that Melissa was looking for constructive feedback so she knew if she was doing well or not and suggested that they meet to review expectations for working together.

Kathleen followed up with Melissa and asked her to suggest ways they could make the process more efficient. With Kathleen's approval, Melissa automated the process and briefed Kathleen on how to generate the reports whenever she wanted hard copies. Because their relationship improved as a result of their communication, Melissa felt comfortable coming to Kathleen as a mentor and about a year later Kathleen recommended her for a promotion.

More to Think About and Try

- We like people who are like us. They "get" our perspective. They agree with our opinions. They're easy to understand. Looking across generations, we see that even though we are from the same place, historical events such as war and the state of the economy have dramatic effects on how each generation interacts with and perceives its world.
- Whether we are young or old, when we work with other generations, we need to take a moment to recognize, appreciate, and leverage, but not criticize, the unique generational characteristics each team member brings to the table.
- Most important, we should recognize what we share: the need for respect, accomplishment, meaning, and individuality.

KEEPING THE BRAIN IN MIND

The link between neuroscience and performance has become a topic of great interest among proactive and engaging supervisors in organizations worldwide.

To influence their staffs to achieve results with efficiency and quality, supervisors today are thinking beyond the traditional approaches. Constant breakthroughs in the field of neuroscience are revealing more about the brain's influence on our behaviors and actions in all areas of performance.

Tom is a new supervisor who has been given the lead on a project that will consume a major portion of his time. The deadline is aggressive and will require his staff to work long days and weekends. Tom worked on intense projects for the first ten years of his career before becoming a supervisor. He knows how to develop a fast-track project schedule that includes status checks to keep on top of progress and obstacles. Tom sets up a schedule that requires frequent meetings and check-ins with key members of the team.

As the project progresses, the staff is attending multiple meetings daily. They are coming in early and leaving very late, putting in 10–14 hours a day. The schedule requires frequent "working" lunches in conference rooms and skipping scheduled breaks. It is common to see people rubbing their eyes during afternoon meetings and forgetting simple details of critical information. The project team is taking longer than usual to make decisions in their meetings—and is scheduling more meetings as a result.

One afternoon, Tom is sitting through his fifth meeting of the day. He needs to be at the top of his game because he will be making a critical presentation to the key project stakeholders in the organization. But the flow of his day has not been conducive to performing at peak: He missed lunch due to a prior meeting; had back-to-back meetings, which left him with no time for a break or to mentally prepare for the presentation; and he had minimal sleep the night before because he was working on several other projects and proposals. The presentation to the stakeholders requires Tom to exhibit alertness, attention to detail, mastery of presentation skills, and flexibility to make last-minute changes linking the most critical project objectives with new organizational strategies.

Stressful situations like this are pretty common across government organizations.

Tom needed to remember to give his brain (and the brains on his team) a break. Until the brain has had a chance to take a break, relax, and store new information in its long-term memory, it is useless to keep taking in information—as a day of one meeting after another demands.

The cost of our failure to understand basic brain function is the steady depletion of resources. Too often, the information that people are expected to absorb in very short timeframes is lost to inefficient brain functioning. Needs go unfulfilled, work is delayed, we lose the ability to grasp new information, and we sacrifice the clear-minded thinking necessary to make important decisions. By not giving our people the opportunity to refresh and rejuvenate their brains, we are actually asking them to do their jobs in an impaired state—and we shouldn't be surprised when the work output suffers.

Prioritizing, organizing, and planning are some of the brain's most taxing, energy-intensive activities. But these daily activities are also extremely critical, allowing us to organize our schedules, plan our weeks, and allocate business resources to meet daily demands and project requirements. Each day, we have to be selective about how we use our limited short-term memory, and we also need to recognize when our brain is becoming fatigued.

If we do not pay attention to the physical signs (such as forgetfulness, cloudy thinking, a hair-trigger temper, the inability to focus), we will find ourselves involuntarily shutting down. We will be wasting time and effort and might find ourselves well on the way toward burnout—in addition to missing project deadlines!

The work environment in most government organizations makes it exceedingly difficult for people to thrive and reach high levels of performance. Traditional organizational norms—which for many supervisors and their teams include high work volumes in a compressed workday with few breaks, no flexibility to attend to personal issues during the day, and the constant demand that work be completed in shorter and shorter timeframes—tend to compromise the brain's ability to function at higher levels.

By keeping the brain in mind, you are applying the knowledge of neuroscience to improve performance.

More to Think About and Try

- *Take breaks.* Allow people to take frequent breaks by doing something fun and energizing. Try to engage in activities that are physically easy and require minimal thought.
- *"Indulge" in brief naps.* Sleep is one of the quickest ways to rejuvenate the brain by freeing up the memory systems to take in more information.
- *Have conversations.* Encourage people to talk about something completely different from the task at hand. Conversations with an informal social aspect can relax the thinking brain and recoup the resources needed to function effectively.
- *Snack on real food.* Provide access to healthy foods and beverages to replenish the glucose burned up in the brain and add protein for sustainability.
- *Laugh more.* Encourage lightness in the work environment to balance the formality of hard-driving tasks. Research shows that fun leads to productivity and also increases the ability to retain important information.

RETOOLING AND REFRESHING TO SET YOURSELF APART

Chris' excitement was through the roof when he learned that he had been promoted. Finally! He was now officially a supervisor of a newly formed team in his agency. Chris felt a quiet confidence in his ability to excel as he emailed his mentor, Soo-Lin, to share the good news with her. After they scheduled their next monthly "coffee talk" meeting, Chris sat at his desk making lists of ideas and action items.

A few weeks later, Soo-Lin relaxed into her chair as she congratulated Chris once again on his accomplishment and listened to his tales of his first month as a supervisor. Sipping her coffee, she listened to his stories of excitement and frustration from her perspective of having been in supervisory roles in the federal government for the past 20 years.

"What are you doing to ramp up your supervisory skills, Chris?" Soo-Lin inquired.

"What do you mean?" asked Chris.

"Well, you have a whole new skill set you need to acquire, and fast. You will certainly learn on the job, but what are you doing to proactively enhance your skills?"

"I'm not sure I have any ideas. What do you suggest?" said Chris, looking at Soo-Lin quizzically.

Over the next hour, Soo-Lin shared with Chris some of the resources that she found helpful, including books, seminars, and training classes. But it was the story she told him that really got Chris thinking about how to keep his skills and knowledge fresh now and into the next stages of his career development.

"You know, when I first got promoted, there were no supervisory training classes offered and no resources given to me to prepare me for my new role. I had to learn as I went, the hard way. Things went very well for the first couple of years and my hard work was rewarded and rewarding.

"But then, things began to shift. I was no longer getting the results I wanted from my staff. They seemed unmotivated and deflated, and I felt frustrated with my job. I applied the same techniques that had worked before, but they were just not working in the same way. I felt really stuck and unhappy. Word got around that there might be a reorganization in our department and I started to worry that I might lose my job.

"That's when I began to realize that I had become stale; my skills and knowledge were not sufficient to produce the performance results I wanted to see. I felt baffled and lost, so I started reading every management book in the library, searching for answers. I also started looking for role models to talk with, both inside and outside my office and agency. I was amazed how happy these successful supervisors were to share their 'best practices' and 'lessons learned' with me, and it was great to learn from them about things I could do or avoid doing—and not have to learn them the hard way! One told me that he attends the monthly meetings of our field's professional association to learn new techniques and connect and network with other professionals with whom he collaborates and shares ideas. So I started attending these meetings also—what an eye-opening experience!

"What I learned, slowly but surely, is that your skills and knowledge need to be constantly upgraded and challenged. You can never rest on your laurels just because you have reached a certain rung on the career ladder; you need to keep working or you'll find yourself falling off—or getting pushed off. And there are so many different ways available to help you retool, refresh, and learn."

This is an exciting time to be a supervisor. You have the opportunity to influence others in a changing landscape. You will be challenged to handle day-to-day issues effectively in the context of an ever-evolving work environment. The best way to create a balance that serves both your employees and your organization well is to keep strengthening your personal capabilities as a supervisor. Only then will you be ready and able to help others envision and prepare to meet the demands of the 21st century government work environment.

More to Think About and Try

- What are some books, training, and other resources you could access to upgrade your supervisory skills? Are there resources that would help you on an ongoing, continuous basis?
- Who are some key people who could help you learn and develop your supervisory skills? Are there any groups you could join or people in your current network you could tap to become your mentors or "master-mind" group?
- Can you branch out and increase your network to include role models and kindred spirits?
- Can you find opportunities to bring supervisors together? Who can—and is willing to—share their lessons learned?

Afterword

Experiences can leave lasting impressions and have lifelong impacts.

Dave was my first government supervisor. His approach to guiding and developing others gave me a starting point for thinking about how I would approach being a supervisor. His positive energy, commitment, and support still influence how I think and act as a supervisor.

Dave asked me to lead a project to set up a new employee orientation program. He shared feedback with me that it was taking too long for people to get through the current process. He challenged me to come up with a program that would help new employees settle into their jobs more quickly and easily. Dave said he could tell I needed more ways to be creative and use my natural leadership skills. He was right, and I had a lot of fun creating the "one-stop" orientation program. Dave provided timely guidance, feedback, and support as I got the program up and running smoothly—making my success possible.

The most important work of a supervisor is to access and multiply the potential of others to make good things happen in organizations.

Throughout *The Insider's Guide to Supervising Government Employees*, we have shared stories about supervisory situations and experiences that shaped the ideas, behaviors, and actions of new and seasoned supervisors. In your quest to be an effective supervisor, you will be well served by applying some of these key learning points:

- Be honest about your readiness to supervise.
- Focus on changing yourself, not others.
- Sense and respond to each work situation by first living within it yourself.
- Openly share your thoughts and ideas; respect the views of others; filter out the noise to get to the heart of the situation.
- Set expectations early and reinforce them over time.
- Be passionate and consistent about your commitment to optimizing available resources.
- Act on the choices you make; step up to difficult decisions or responsibilities; create small, achievable wins.
- Recognize others for accomplishing good things.
- Keep learning and growing to be at your best; use your supervisory experiences to recognize your own truths about being a supervisor.

Being an effective supervisor is the most important job in all of government. By making good things happen through others, you multiply the effects of your work. As a government supervisor, you have incalculable influence on the values, perspectives, work activities, engagement, and organizational alignment of others. The choice is yours to create a positive or negative experience for others.

What kind of lasting impression and long-term impact do you want to have as a government supervisor? Seize the opportunity and step up to make good things happen!

About the Contributors

Heidi T. Alt has been a supervisor for 10 years. She currently supervises a team of cross-channel marketing specialists in advertising, graphic and web design, electronic media, and event planning.

Julia Anderson has worked on education, training, and workforce issues in both the public and private sectors, supervising three to over 100 employees. She has a master's degree in Social Foundations of Education from the University of Virginia.

Halelly Azulay is a professional leadership facilitator and consultant who has performed in management, supervisory, and team leader roles as well as led volunteers. She works with leaders and teams to improve the human side of work in public, private, and nonprofit organizations.

Barbara Kres Beach is the executive director of external and strategic relations for a training, performance, and publishing organization; she works to serve the public at the intersection of federal, nonprofit, and private-sector organizations. She has launched and led two NGOs and serves as director of three.

Ken Buch is a certified trainer, facilitator, consultant, and executive coach who has worked in transportation, telecommunications, banking, and the federal government. He received his master's degree in organization development and human resources from Johns Hopkins University. He also holds certifications as a Fellow in the Management of Change from Johns Hopkins University and Leadership Coaching from Georgetown University.

Briana Colescott has more than 20 years of supervisory experience. She has managed a case load of developmentally disabled adults in a sheltered work environment, a team of administrative support staff in the nonprofit educational arena, a team of training delivery resources within the telecommunications industry, and training and professional services engagements for both federal and private-sector clients.

Shelly Cook has led services support teams for over 10 years. She is instrumental in driving continuous improvement activities that impact cost, quality, and delivery of consulting and training services.

Mary Cowell is a publishing executive who creates informational resources for the federal government. She is committed to advancing thought leadership in the public sector and increasing the level of professionalism among government supervisors.

Tom Dausch has held management and supervisory positions for more than 30 years. He has managed both headquarters and field operations for the federal government and has directed key business units for professional services companies.

Judith Dickinson has management and training experience in Fortune 100 technology, financial services, and Big 4 consulting firms. She has earned the Senior Professional in Human Resources credential and is a certified Project Management Professional.

Mickey Donovan specializes in designing and delivering customized training, coaching, and consultative problem solving. She supervised 10 consultants as they rolled out a nationwide series of courses she had developed for two Fortune 500 Network Systems Call Center Operations. She is an experienced facilitator in federal and commercial organizations.

Flip Filippi has spent most of the past 31 years in a variety of leadership positions with formal supervisory responsibilities. In his 25 years in the military, he has been a commander and director leading organizations with as few as five persons and as many as 850. He currently advises leaders on how to handle a variety of supervisory challenges.

Tanya Griffey has worked for the U.S. Army–Europe and has served as a U.S. Peace Corps Advanced Business Volunteer in Kazakhstan. She has experience managing projects in the aerospace, adult education, and hospitality marketing industries and is a certified Project Management Professional.

Rebecca James served in various supervisory roles in the field of education, including team lead, mentor, and assistant principal. Throughout those years, she focused on strategic planning, professional development, and performance monitoring. She is currently an instructional designer of courses in supervision, leadership, and professional skills.

Anne Kelly has 20 years of senior leadership experience in two federal agencies. She has managed a diverse workforce, ranging from administrative staff to attorneys, engineers, and senior executives. She attributes her skills in engaging employees and being able to deliver effective feedback to real-time learning, good advice from mentors, and trial and error.

Shelley A. Kirkpatrick, Ph.D., has managed research and assessment teams for over 20 years, focusing on developing individual and organizational assessments for the private sector as well as national security and defense organizations. She holds a Ph.D. in organizational behavior and human resource management.

Catherine A. Kreyche supervises a product development and services delivery team. She also gives conference presentations on worklife and professional challenges.

Kathleen Mahoney Landerholm is the managing editor of a variety of technical publications geared toward the federal sector. She has several years of supervisory experience.

Mark Leheney has supervised employees in the United States and Europe in a financial information organization. He currently coaches supervisors and managers and conducts leadership and supervisory training for government employees. He holds a master's degree in Organization Development and Knowledge Management and is an ICF-certified coach. He is the author of the book *The Five Commitments of a Leader*.

Susan Levin is a facilitator, trainer, coach, and mediator. For more than 20 years, she has worked with thousands of employees from a variety of organizations in the United States and abroad. She focuses on maximizing individual and organizational strengths to bring out the most effective skills and approaches.

Warren Master is president and editor-at-large of *The Public Manager*. A former Peace Corps volunteer in Turkey, he served as a frontline supervisor and senior executive in the U.S. government, holding a variety of field operations, policy, and administrative management posts during his 30-year federal career.

Anna Mauldin gained her supervisory experience in both small businesses and large companies. She currently applies her supervisory knowledge and experience as an instructional designer of government and commercial leadership and management programs.

Kathryn Mooney has supervised teams and multimillion-dollar projects in the financial asset management industry. She earned her MBA, with a focus on Leadership and Organizational Development, from the Robert H. Smith School of Business at the University of Maryland.

Cristine Offutt, CPA, has spent much of her career in finance and accounting in the government contracting industry. She has over 20 years of supervisory experience.

Cleve Pillifant has more than 30 years of experience in systems analysis, process improvement, government accounting systems and practices, business planning, and major system program management. A Level III-certified Defense Acquisition Professional in business and cost estimating, he has extensive experience with all branches of the military services.

Cristina Rodarte has taught English as a Foreign Language in France and Chile. She has also worked as an adjunct professor and as a program assistant to international students in the United States.

John Salamone has nearly 20 years of experience managing people, projects, and processes as a federal government employee and consultant. He is currently managing five federal projects as a consultant with over 20 staff and has six direct reports on his team.

Daniel M. Soderberg has 29 years in military and civilian service to the government. He has developed his supervisory style through a variety of roles and responsibilities.

Robin Sparks blends direct experience supervising and leading others with hands-on expertise in leadership and management development, employee training, and curriculum design and development. She also serves as an executive coach and program manager on a variety of organizational performance and deve-lopment issues, with emphasis on employee satisfaction and engagement, organizational culture, performance management, and the development of leaders at all levels.

Larry Walters started out working for a large government contractor and then moved to supervision in the private healthcare industry. For the past 20 years he has supervised technical staff for dot coms and private companies.

Casey Wilson has direct supervisory experience in government, not-for-profit, and commercial industries. He is currently a practice director for a leadership and management group. His recent book, *The Cornerstones of Engaging Leadership,* helps leaders and managers more effectively engage others to increase workplace satisfaction and results. He facilitates training that includes building high-performance teams, performance management, and human resource management.

Catherine Zaranis has supervised account managers in consulting with clients on financial and political factors affecting the foreign currency markets and suggesting hedging strategies to protect their bottom line. She is currently responsible for identifying the training and development needs of public and private sector organizations. She has served as a Peace Corps volunteer in Romania.

Introducing ... The Practical Leader Series!

Offering a roadmap to achieving leadership effectiveness in today's complex world, each book in this series explores a different essential element of successful leadership. This series provides insightful, real-world perspectives, as well as practical tools and techniques to help readers maximize their potential—personally and professionally.

BONUS! Each book comes with a CD-ROM offering additional tools, techniques, exercises, and other resources to help readers become effective leaders.

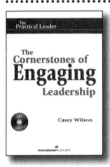

The Cornerstones of Engaging Leadership
Casey Wilson
The Cornerstones of Engaging Leadership connects what we know about engagement on an organizational level to what an individual leader can do to increase engagement. Using real-world examples, author Casey Wilson reveals the key actions leaders must take to connect with and engage others—build trust, leverage unique motivators, manage performance from a people-centric perspective, and engage emotions. By committing to these four cornerstones of engaging leadership, leaders can unleash the potential of others and inspire effective performance.
ISBN 978-1-56726-218-6 ■ Product Code B186 ■ 151 pages

The Five Commitments of a Leader
Mark Leheney
In ***The Five Commitments of a Leader***, author Mark Leheney presents a revealing way to examine leadership—through the commitments a leader makes (or fails to make). He focuses on five commitments a leader must make to be effective—commitments to the self, people, the organization, the truth, and leadership. Leheney challenges leaders to understand stated versus actual commitments, and through self-assessment and practice tools, he encourages leaders to ask themselves accountability-creating questions.
ISBN 978-1-56726-219-3 ■ Product Code B193 ■ 160 pages

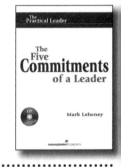

Anytime Coaching: Unleashing Employee Performance
Teresa Wedding Kloster and Wendy Sherwin Swire
Anytime Coaching: Unleashing Employee Performance is a practical guide to putting coaching skills to use any time. Learning from real-life stories, simple tips and techniques, and the Anytime Coaching model, managers ranging from first-time supervisors to senior executives will be equipped with a set of coaching tools they can use immediately to transform the way they work with employees and colleagues—unleashing their best thinking and growing their overall competence.
ISBN 978-1-56726-237-7 ■ Product Code B377 ■ 182 pages

Order today for a 30-day risk-free trial!
Visit **www.managementconcepts.com/pubs** or call **800-506-4450**